W9-CCC-610

HELP!
for
WRITERS

Books by Roy Peter Clark

Writing Tools
The Glamour of Grammar

HELP!

for

WRITERS

HELP!

for

WRITERS

210 SOLUTIONS TO THE PROBLEMS

EVERY WRITER FACES

ROY PETER CLARK

LITTLE, BROWN AND COMPANY
NEW YORK   BOSTON   LONDON

Little, Brown and Company
Hachette Book Group
237 Park Avenue, New York, NY 10017
www.hachettebookgroup.com

First Edition: September 2011

Little, Brown and Company is a division of Hachette Book Group, Inc.
The Little, Brown name and logo are trademarks of Hachette Book Group, Inc.

The publisher is not responsible for websites (or their content)
that are not owned by the publisher.

Thanks to Rochelle Kraut for permission to reprint her poem "My Makeup."
Thanks to author Jack Riston for permission to quote from
his website: www.jackriston.com.

Library of Congress Cataloging-in-Publication Data
Clark, Roy Peter.
    Help! for writers: 210 solutions to the problems every writer faces /
by Roy Peter Clark. — 1st ed.
    p. cm.
    Includes index.
    ISBN 978-0-316-12671-7
    1. English language — Rhetoric.   2. Report writing.   I. Title.
PE1404.C54 2011
808'.042 — dc22   2011004683

10   9   8   7   6   5   4   3   2   1

RRD-C

Printed in the United States of America

To my mother and first editor:

Shirley Hope Marino Clark

Contents

—•—

Making it better

Completing a draft of a text can be such hard work that the writer may be charmed by the illusion that the job is almost finished. But the process does not stop there. The final problem for the writer is how and what to revise, what to delete, what to insert. It is during revision that the writer will refine, polish, and perfect a work that can never be perfect but can grow and become good enough to fulfill the writer's purpose. Key to a successful endgame is to leave time and energy for revision, the way a long-distance runner saves energy for a sprint to the finish line.

Get started
Get your act together
Find focus
Look for language
Build a draft
Assess your progress
Make it better

If those seven phrases represent the writer's largest and most imposing tasks, the effort to complete them can be stymied by a set of pesky problems. Those problems have influenced the structure of *Help!* Each chapter begins with an explanation of one stage of the writing process, followed by questions for reflection. At each stage you will encounter three of the most persistent and difficult obstacles to completing that task, a total of twenty-one common writing problems. For each problem, I offer ten practical and proven solutions, drawn from the work and life stories of successful writers, living and dead. Do the math (even you English majors) and realize you own the 210 writing solutions promised on the cover, enough life-lines to survive a mudslide of deadlines.

—•—

The Seven Steps of the Writing Process

Writing is not magic. It's a craft, a process, a set of steps. As with any process, things sometimes break down. Even in a good story, the writer runs into problems. So the act of writing always includes problem solving. At times, things get so bad, writers feel as if they're drowning. Before going under, they reach for a lifeline.

This book offers that lifeline.

To hear some writers talk, you would think we have problems in the gajillions, from whether to use *gajillion* or *gazillion*, to whether that exclamation point after *Help* is necessary.

As I've grown in my own craft, I've listened to my brothers and sisters of the word and have developed a theory to focus this book. Here it is, my Theory of Writer Redemption: *The big problems of writers are few in number and lend themselves to reliable solutions.* I subscribe to the gospel of Donald Murray, one of America's most influential writing teachers, that writers — across genres and disciplines — share a similar process, a set of tactical steps. If you dig deep enough, you can discover that common method.

Surely, you wonder, the sonneteer must develop a different approach to the craft than the pamphleteer? How about the author of a 140-character message on Twitter? Is her process the same as the novelist's? At the highest level of abstraction, my answer would be yes.

So what are those shared steps?

Getting started

All writers need a kick start, a starter's pistol, a spur to the flank, something that jolts them into action. This recurring need leads them to explore the world and their own experiences for writing ideas. Such curiosity turns them into hunters and gatherers who collect the raw materials that render their reports and stories interesting and significant.

Getting your act together

A writer who goes exploring can bring home so many treasures that the writing space and the writer's mind can become cluttered. Writers must be able to find *what* they need *when* they need it. At this stage, it is too early to know whether an author has what she needs to fill a novel or memoir or annual report with interesting and important ideas, facts, and language.

Finding focus

Each piece of writing benefits from a focus, a guiding idea, a scene, or an emotion that communicates to writer and reader what the work is really about. A telegram, Twitter post, or haiku needs a focus, but so does a short story, a love note, or a complaint about your plumber to the Better Business Bureau. Such a unifying notion helps the writer select the best collected material—the best characters, the best details, the most important points, down to the best word and the best mark of punctuation. A focus will help the writer craft an opening sentence or paragraph; and sometimes writing that paragraph is required to find a focus. It's the yin/yang of the writing process.

Looking for language

The Old English poets were said to have a "word hoard" from which they could choose the best language to shape their poems. How great it would be to throw open a closet door and find just the right word for just the right writing task. Where do such words come from? They come from a life of reading and study of the craft, from the daily experience of language, from travel, from dictionaries, and from the research required to gather not just raw data but the ideas, images, and key words necessary to understand a group of people or a field of study.

Building a draft

It is never easy to know when it's time to sit down at your keyboard to create a first draft. The writer often feels resistance at this stage, expressed as writer's block or procrastination. The writing will begin to flow if the writer has attended to the earlier steps. W. H. Auden once described a poem as a "verbal contraption" with a person, a guiding intelligence, hiding inside. All texts are constructed, often from a blueprint or plan, erecting an architecture of meaning and purpose. The writer must decide on a sequence — what goes first in a work and what goes last. A haiku has three lines, a legal brief builds an argument, Shakespeare wrote plays in five acts and sonnets in fourteen lines. Each part of the work carries a special power, magnified when the writer creates an effective structure for the whole.

Assessing your progress

When writers talk to teachers or editors, they often blurt blurry language to mask the one key question that concerns them: "How am I doing?" As a coach, my version of that question, as I approach a writer, is "How is it going?" Everyone wants a progress report, calibrated against different goals and criteria. The writer makes preliminary judgments about the current quality of the work and how much time and energy are left to improve it. The writer can reach conclusions on his own but often benefits from an intervention. When Donald Murray was asked how the day's writing had gone, he had two reliable answers, both framed in the affirmative. He could respond by quantity: "I produced ten pages before lunch." Or, if necessary, by quality: "I wrote one really great sentence this morning."

...you can't decide what to include and what to leave
out, or

...you think your last paragraph should be your first, or

...you begin to wonder why you became a writer in the
first place.

You realize you need help. In fact, you realize you need
Help!

This book offers a road map to get you through your writing process, a travel guide that takes you from the exploration of story ideas to the final choices of revision. But it would be a mistake to think of writing as a straight and narrow road, or this book as some program of recovery for drunken drivers that must be followed one step after another. The writing process more resembles a twisting mountain roadway where solutions for your next problem can be found back a few miles. For that reason, we have built into *Help!* a certain amount of strategic repetition. You'll discover, for example, that the idea of *setting an early artificial deadline* works at almost every stage of the process, through research, planning, drafting, and revision.

It should be a comfort for you to learn that the problems of writers (and drivers!) are predictable and manageable. So click on your seatbelt. Turn the ignition key. Let's get started. And enjoy the ride.

How to Get *Help!*

—•—

Feel free to think of *Help! For Writers* as an owner's manual for your writing process. When I bought my 2002 Chrysler PT Cruiser, my first job was to read the owner's manual from beginning to end, just to get the lay of the automotive land. I don't remember consulting it again until the evening a neighbor knocked to alert me that my dome light was on, draining my battery. I tried the usual fixes: flicking switches, checking fuses, slamming doors. Nothing worked. I was stuck. What could I do? "Why don't you consult the owner's manual," said my wife with grumpy disdain.

All writers live for those days when the work speeds along the highway on cruise control, when the author's only tasks are to point the hood ornament toward the destination and steer. But then there are those days when...

  ... you can't get started, or
  ... you can't find something you need amid all your
      clutter, or

—•—

Getting Started

Having the urge to write is one thing; acting on it is another. At the age of fifteen, I broke my ankle during a baseball game, and I still remember how I planned my first week of recovery. I would write a spy novel. It was the era of *Goldfinger* and *Thunderball,* and I dreamed of creating my own version of superspy 007. I was a good and clever writer as a teenager but had written nothing longer than a short story or a book report. No matter. I was ready to go. I found a comfortable spot on the back porch, rested my bum leg on a cushion, grabbed a legal pad and ballpoint pen, and then...nothing.

I have a clear memory of what stopped me from getting started: I did not know *how* to write a novel. I knew what a novel looked like, but not the process needed to create one. I thought I could write a book just by milking my imagination. After all, it was fiction. I could invent stuff. But it soon became clear that I needed to know more, a lot more—about spies, about Russians, about gadgets, about women, about everything—before I could proceed. Then the doubts arrived: "What made you think you could write a novel? You're not a writer. You're just a clumsy little asshole. You can't even slide into home plate without breaking an ankle."

Then, of course, the temptations followed: "Roy, the Yankees game is on. Wanna come in and watch it?" "Hey, kid, want to go to Carvel for some ice cream?" "Hey, Roy, Rosie's on the phone for you."

We learn in science class that *inertia* is a physical force that manifests itself in two ways. Things that are still—not moving—will stay still until acted upon by outside forces. (My laptop will remain on my desk until I pick it up and fling it—discus-style—out the window.) But inertia also describes the way an object in motion *stays* in motion until some external force slows or stops it. For the purposes of writing, I call the first kind "bad inertia" because it describes inactive writers who can't get moving. The other kind is "good inertia," because once you get started you can keep things rolling. No writing creates no writing. Some writing creates more writing. Getting started requires forms of exploration that become a way of life. The writer is a curious person who discovers topics to write about and, over time, comes to see the world as a storehouse of story ideas. Just as Rex, my little terrier, goes out into the yard to sniff for possums, so the writer is ignited by the hint of something in the air, a thought, a theory, an emotion, a story, a character worth attention, a problem to be solved.

Problems covered in this chapter:

NO IDEAS

The first challenge is to find something to write about. In my experience, there are two basic types of writers: the ones who write only in response to assignments and those who find ways to work on their own story ideas. Writers need both modes to fulfill the demands of the craft, but the best writers follow their noses along the path to good stories. They generate many more ideas than can be put into practice. That's a nice problem to have. No writer should descend into a welfare system provided by editors or teachers or bosses. The writer wants and needs the ability to work independently. That means coming up with your own ideas and arguing diplomatically that your ideas have the best juice.

BAD ASSIGNMENTS

There are no bad story ideas or bad story assignments. What turns out to be good or bad is what the writer does with the idea or assignment. The assignment is a starting point. Editors or teachers may disagree, especially those who insist on adding stipulations for its execution: "You've got to cover the meeting, get responses from each member of the city council, three reactions from people who live on the north side of town, three from the south side..." In such cases, the writer feels like a short-order cook. With enough freedom, the writer explores the assignment for the elements that will be most interesting and most important, being alert to those sudden moments of clarity when even a bad assignment becomes a nifty story.

TROUBLE WITH RESEARCH

If your goal is to write a book, research may take years or even decades. Or, if an emergency call comes in and you must verify whether the fire destroyed the friary or the nunnery, it can take five minutes. Writers make the mistake of thinking of writing and research as mutually exclusive tasks. Since the research usually comes first, it can grow bigger and bigger, feeding on time that could be spent on drafting and revision. A reliable strategy is to write early and often, even if just a note on the results of the day's research. Writing about your research will help you determine whether you know enough to write at full speed or need to learn much more.

REFLECT

Here and throughout the book, use the following questions to better understand yourself as a writer. Think about them. Talk about them with teachers, editors, students, friends, other writers. Write down your reflections and save them. Go back to them down the road and discover how far you have traveled.

- Do you think of yourself as curious?
- When was the last time you were dying to find out something about a person or a place?
- Are you more likely to get story impulses, ideas, or assignments?

- When was the last time you thought of a great writing idea?
- What are some of the things you do now to find great stories?
- What's the most interesting thing about you that others do not know?
- How much of your writing time is spent on research?
- What do you find most interesting or most frustrating about research?

1

——•——

I can't think of anything to write.

Spend a morning in a bagel shop or an afternoon in a bookstore.

For the price of a cup of coffee and a bagel, you can listen in on the morning's conversations about news and current events; or you can browse through new books and magazines at a favorite bookstore. A survey will generate an endless stream of story ideas. Any café or bookstore is a story idea machine.

I just spent twenty minutes with the magazines displayed in the library of the Poynter Institute, the school where I've taught writing for more than thirty years. Even with our focus on journalism, I found an array of topics in the cover stories alone, gaining an overview of the broad concerns of the day. In April 2010 these included health care reform, how to survive in a bad economy, the influence of the iPad and other reading tablets, attempts to deal with childhood obesity, the beginning of baseball season, the Tiger Woods sex scandal. Within this forest of large issues, interesting little stories hide behind the trees. (For example, I'm thinking of writing a comparison of the Apple iPad with the classic kid's toy Etch A Sketch.)

My eyes found the cover of *Publishers Weekly,* which included this tease: "Dystopian Future Is Here: Teens are reading about vampires, but end-of-the world scenarios are bigger than ever." A light flickered in my head. What, I wondered, is the relationship between vampire stories and narratives about the end of the world, and is there any link to the fact that we have begun calling some young people "millennials"? Suddenly, I'm off and running—and writing.

Keep a little notebook to compile story ideas.

Ideas can be elusive—like fireflies at dusk. You will need a dozen story ideas for every one you eventually execute. You'll need a place to store them. Use whatever suits you, including the notes mode on your mobile phone. I prefer to go old-school: a tiny notebook suitable for pocket or purse. I know writers who need paper in their pockets, in their cars, on the toilet tank, on the table beside their beds. The eccentric artist Salvador Dalí was known to take quick naps and awaken suddenly, his head filled with surrealistic images. He would capture these images on a pad as soon as possible so that they could not escape.

Your notebook can contain fully articulated story ideas, such as "Sports journalists and the public are harsher in their criticism of women athletes who play aggressively—to the point of violence—than of male athletes." More often, you will record the seeds of story ideas, most of which will die out. A few will bear fruit. Here are examples of seedlings:

- Not one person played an April Fool's joke on me this year.
- Does the word *dope,* as in the Disney dwarf Dopey, derive from the slang word for drugs? (Turned out the drug slang derives from the Dutch word for sauce or gravy.)
- Saw ten big alligators around the golf course. What's the rule for a ball that's in play but dangerously close to a gator? ("Dogleg to the left; gator jaws to the right!")
- Church was packed for Easter Sunday Mass, but saw only three Easter bonnets, all worn by little girls. Whither the bonnet?

Read a book on a topic that is unfamiliar to you.

Insomnia can be good for you. It was good for me one night when, at about three A.M., I got up and turned on the television to see a C-SPAN panel featuring the work of Timothy Ferris, author of several important books on astronomy and cosmology. No, not cosmetology. That deals with craters on your skin. Ferris is more interested in craters on the moon and one, about a hundred miles wide, off the Mexican coast, possibly responsible for the extinction of many species on earth, including the dinosaurs.

See how much I've learned just by watching, and then reading, Ferris? You should always have "a book going," advised Donald Murray, that comes from outside your normal field of interest. Because my interests are reading, writing, sports, and language, my "outside" reading includes works on photography and the visual arts, philosophy and theology, natural science, and applied mathematics. By reading such work, I discover not just specialized content but also story ideas that span more than one field.

You don't have to spend much money. New media technologies afford access to texts of all genres, from all disciplines, written over centuries. Through online bookstores alone, writers can read passages — for free — of books that are for sale. Research is not the primary purpose of such commercial enterprises, but they allow us to taste many books and articles, including the ones we will one day purchase.

Break your routine. Go to work or school a different way.

I am a creature of routine, especially when it comes to my personal life. I like to stay home and watch television on Friday nights. And I enjoy going to breakfast on Saturday morning at the Frog Pond restaurant, especially if they are serving strawberry waffles. That doesn't mean I have to drive to the restaurant the same way each week, and I try not to. There are probably ten or more routes from my house to St. Pete Beach, and I've taken most of them.

You may see stories from the vantage point of the main road: construction of a new big-box store, which might bring more traffic and more congestion — but lower prices. A great offbeat story, on the other hand, is more likely to be found on a side street, off the beaten path. An eagle sits atop a light pole, looking down at children playing soccer. An eighty-year-old Catholic nun takes dance lessons from a former Rockette. A charter school for poor kids offers golf lessons for PE. A corner of a cemetery is reserved for stillborn children. None of this is visible from the main road, so you must learn to turn left, turn right, and drive down that alley, even if it takes you a little longer to reach your destination.

There are stories that come out of Wall Street and others that come out of Main Street, but don't get stuck in that false dichotomy. There are many stories to be found on the side streets and especially, as Bruce Springsteen reminds us, on the backstreets.

Eat out.

In the last couple of years, I have switched my lunch place of choice from Pizza Hut to the Banyan restaurant and coffee shop. The Banyan is more stylish but sits across the alley from Molly's, a rooming house and bar that features a Laundromat and draft beer for a dollar. Negotiating the distance between those two unlikely neighbors, I'm sure I've run into dozens of story ideas, most of which I would never have encountered had I not abandoned my personal pan pizza routine.

Francis X. Clines, one of the finest writers in the history of the *New York Times,* once said that he knew he could find a good story if he could just get out of the office. With a virtual world at their fingertips, writers seem more office bound than ever. Achieving escape velocity from a mediated world to a flesh-and-blood one takes a concerted effort.

When people eat, they also laugh, argue, canoodle, whisper, check each other out, check you out, or talk too loud. Enjoy your meal but keep that mobile device in your pocket or purse and focus your attention on what is going on around you. Never be afraid to turn your listening into a conversation, especially with an interesting stranger.

There are eight million stories in the naked city, said the narrator of the old television series. Even better, there are at least three or four in a local eatery, if you can just get out of the office, or off campus, or even down the street. The school or office cafeteria may crave your business — or you may prefer a peanut butter and jelly sandwich at your desk — but your physical liberation from such cloisters will lead you to a world of stories.

Watch people in their natural habitats.

My cousin Theresa was high up in the World Trade Center when the first plane hit her building on the morning of September 11, 2001. She hadn't had breakfast yet, so she was about to enjoy a muffin and cup of coffee with her coworkers. They all felt the impact of the plane, and the whole building seemed to sway back and forth, a cart of fruit rolling first to the left, then to the right, and back to the left. She escaped with her life, but nothing would be the same for any of us.

This may be the ultimate example of what screenwriter Robert McKee describes as an "inciting incident," an event, small or large, that dramatically changes the nature of an ordinary day, that "radically upsets the balance of forces in the protagonist's life." Anyone who has been in a car accident knows the feeling. Just another day of work, a routine drive down the service road of a busy highway, and then WHAM. We have a cliché to describe such events. We say they hit us "out of the blue."

Before we can tell stories about these lightning strikes, we have to develop a keen sense of normal life. How were people acting in the bar and grill at the exact moment that the runaway car crashed through the picture window? One way to learn the narrative potential of normal experience is to hang out. Where? In a sense, it does not matter: Try the park, the mall, a busy street, the gym, a hotel lobby, a church, a concert hall, a pub, the airport, the bleachers during a high school football game, Dunkin' Donuts. Ride the bus. Take the train. Even when you are stuck inside that human sardine can we call an airplane, take in the setting. Imagine that a scene will play out there. Watch people's reaction upon takeoff, or when the first bump of turbulence strikes. Could you write a play from the dialogue between characters on that plane—or a novel?

Your body may just be hanging out in all these places, but your mind is on fire with curiosity, imagining character, dialogue, narrative tension, points of view, a sequence of scenes— all the building blocks of story construction.

Read posters, billboards, store signs, graffiti.

Lane DeGregory, one of the most talented narrative writers in America, offers this advice to fledgling scribes: "Let the walls talk." Drive around and look at the big signs, commercial and governmental. Walk around to see what the small signs say. When you enter a building or an office or someone's home, look at what they've hung up on the walls or, especially, on the refrigerator door. In our house, that door will have a lot to say: You'll find newspaper clippings about our daughter's theatrical performances, the names of local businesses we support, magnets with the names of products or causes, funny stories or comic strips to which we relate, crucial telephone numbers, a recipe that signals an upcoming holiday feast. If you write fiction, you have many important scenic decisions to make, including "What will the walls say about my characters?"

I once shadowed a political writer, Howell Raines, to a barbecue in rural Florida, and we wandered through the parking lot, looking at the bumper stickers. Howell wanted the car bumpers to talk to him about the political, religious, and cultural affiliations of those in attendance. "Let me know if you see any 'George Wallace for President' signs," he coached me.

If you were writing a story about me, you could learn a lot by letting my office walls and shelves talk. You would see a campaign poster from the 1930s of my grandfather Peter Marino, who ran as a Republican for the New York State Assembly. Next to it, you can find his name as a four-year-old boy on a ship's manifest from about 1900 that records his family's journey from Italy to the Port of New York. You'll find a small black-and-white sports pennant with the name of my alma mater, Providence. You'll find a photo of me as a young child typing on a toy typewriter. There is an artistic representation of my boyhood sports hero (Mickey Mantle) standing next to my mother's idol (Joe DiMaggio). Twenty minutes in my office will have the walls not just talking but shouting details about my family history and my values.

Read the news for undeveloped story ideas.

By now all fans of TV's *Law & Order* understand that many of the story lines are "ripped from the headlines." I guess when you've been on the air for so many years—and spawned so many spin-offs—you'd better have a convenient way to generate plots, and what better place to find them than in the news? Begin with the small stories, the ones inside the paper. Look for announcements of events you might write about. Scour the classified ads, in the paper and online. Check out the list of lost puppies.

I remember well the day I noticed an announcement on the religion page of the newspaper that a young minister was going to spend the weekend on a platform atop a tall pole and preach the gospel to all who would listen. The item made me recall the story of a famous hermit from the early Christian church, Simeon Stylites, who lived and prayed and preached from atop a pillar.

When I traveled to the city of Bradenton to interview the preacher, I noticed how many Protestant churches stood on the street where he worked: at least six or seven, as I recall. Then it struck me. These churches competed for congregants and their souls. Each needed a way to stand out, and what better way to stand out than from atop a pole? Marketing the gospel from on high.

Here is the first item in the Lost column of today's classified ads: "Bird — Cockatiel, grey with white face. St. Pete Beach area. Whistles at toes! Heartbroken [Phone number]." It took me thirty seconds to find the telephone number of a person who lives on the beach and is heartbroken because his cockatiel — who whistles at toes — is missing. So what are you waiting for? Get to work. Dial that number.

(There is an epilogue to this anecdote. On my tip, the *St. Petersburg Times* profiled the poor man who had lost his feathered friend. A few days later, the bird was spotted in a tropical storm and rescued by Vanessa Tonelli, who returned it to its grateful owner. Coincidentally, I've known Vanessa since she was a little girl. See, this stuff works!)

Interview the oldest person you know, and the youngest.

Many people are living longer and healthier lives. Someone who was born in 1919, like my mother, has experienced the

Depression, World War II, the invention of the television, the fall of Soviet Russia, the election of an African American president, and on and on. Such human sources are precious—and fleeting. They provide testimony for oral histories, and they embody a set of experiences that can be mined for story ideas, both fiction and nonfiction. Tommy Carden died at the age of eighty-one, but not before I had an opportunity to extract his memories of the invasion of Normandy, the Battle of the Bulge, and the liberation of Buchenwald concentration camp.

A friend once referred to me as an "anniversarist," and it's true. The recurring cycle of time—often expressed as an anniversary—offers opportunities to learn about the past, and to see our history as a mirror of our own time and place. This book, I just realized, is scheduled for publication the month of the tenth anniversary of 9/11/2001. A few years ago we recognized in St. Petersburg the hundredth anniversary of the birth of Salvador Dalí (St. Pete has a Dalí museum). By August I will have been married forty years to the same woman. Look for such anniversaries as an opportunity to find sources who lived through the original events.

While wisdom, at least on occasion, comes with age, it can also come with youth, and even kids can become sources for story ideas. Like others of my age, I often ask for practical advice from children on how to play a video game or how to put other technologies to work. I recently discovered that a five-year-old boy named Donovan is an expert on all things *Star Wars*. (He hit me in the knee with his version of a lightsaber—and left a mark.) And my little next-door neighbor, a five-year-old girl named Charlie, stood in my driveway yesterday, turned, looked in to where I was working, and said, "Wow, Mr. Clark. Nice garage!"

Spend the day with a person whose job interests you.

A classic example of an offbeat story idea was carried out by columnist and author Jimmy Breslin, who, on the day of John F. Kennedy's burial at Arlington Cemetery in 1963, wrote a story about the grave-digger. If you can't think of anything else to write, go spend a day with a grave-digger.

Jeff Klinkenberg has built his career as a Florida feature writer with an eye for eccentric characters performing quirky jobs. In four anthologies of his work, you can find a sponge diver, a plume hunter, a hog catcher, the original Coppertone girl, a highway patrolman, a fish smoker, a taxidermist, and a Holocaust survivor turned burlesque queen who now repairs roofs on apartments she owns.

There may be no more reliable story form than "a day in the life." The "day" part of this equation creates an immediate time element that places useful boundaries around the research and spins possible narrative lines for a story. And the "life" part allows the writer to see sources in their natural habitats, observing them in action rather than interviewing them in stasis. It also helps to find a person who works as close to the action as possible: the garbage truck driver, not the supervisor; the prostitute, not the madam; the grave-digger, not the cemetery director.

2

—•—

I hate writing assignments and other people's ideas.

Learn to turn an assignment into your story.

This strategy may persuade you that the stories generated by your own ideas can be as good as or better than the stories that come from assignments. The reason is obvious: When we invest in something, we treasure it more. That is true whether the investment is in a mortgage (which, by the way, once meant "death oath"), a marriage, or a common stock. You care more when it's your idea; when you care more, you try harder. You try harder to validate the reason you went after the story in the first place. From your view of the world, *this* is what matters; this idea is interesting and important.

These feelings can have dangerous consequences. You cannot be a writer and believe that only your ideas are worthwhile. Talk with your editor, teacher, friend, or coworker. Find out what potential that person sees in the assignment. Holster your gun and proceed with a sincere desire to learn. But remember this: You are not on the job to dish out whatever greasy meal the boss orders. Good work requires you to test the assumptions built into any idea. The assignment may be to find out why there are so many auto accidents along Route 19, but your research may show that the statistics are skewed by trouble at one particular intersection. The assignment may have come from someone else, but you can turn it into *your* story.

Treat assignments as story topics rather than story ideas.

Remember that "Write something about Mother's Day" is only a topic or occasion, not a full-grown story idea. The key choices remain with you, including whether to write about mothers, grandmothers, or great-grandmothers; you could write about the Mother Superior who works at the Mother House. You could write, as Lane DeGregory did, about a frat house mother who had no children of her own. If you really want to go around the bend, write about the "yo mama" jokes used in humorous insult fights. One of the Ten Commandments orders us to honor our mothers, so what's up with "Yo mama so stank she makes Right Guard turn left and Secret tell all"?

Writers take pleasure from finding an alternate route to a great story. One of my favorite opportunities arrived when the identity of the man who helped Woodward and Bernstein bring down Richard Nixon was finally revealed. For thirty years we knew that mysterious person (W. Mark Felt) as Deep Throat, based on a famous pornographic movie from the early 1970s. It occurred to me that while the deep background source may have helped expose government secrets, it was the movie that would have the more sustained influence on American culture. The movie, I argued, led to the "pornographication" of many aspects of our national identity. When all the other writers are looking at the stage, don't be afraid to turn around and watch the audience.

Make it your own.

This is one of the tired pieces of advice that TV judges give to contestants in talent shows such as *American Idol*. "You did it just like the record, dawg. You got to find a way to make it your own."

Many high school graduations are written about in formulaic ways. But each ceremony has its special feel, and the attentive writer has the ability to capture that in the writing. At my daughter Lauren's graduation in 1999, a late-afternoon Florida storm threatened to drown out the event, the wind knocking over portable chairs on the football field and sending mortarboards spinning across the campus like tumbleweeds. As the ceremony went on for an hour, then two, apocalyptic storm clouds shrouded the eastern sky and began to drift over the stadium. In a visually stunning juxtaposition, the western sky revealed a spectacular sunset, with hints of a rainbow forming in the distance.

These narrative details add value to a piece of writing. My story would have the important facts and details, of course: the number of graduates, the names of valedictorian and salutatorian, two or three key thematic quotes from speakers. But if I had my way, all that would be encased in a gorgeous setting that reflected my voice as a writer and what it was really like to be there. (Years later, we still talk about that stormy rite of passage.)

Send up a flare to express dissatisfaction with an assignment or to suggest something better.

Be direct with an editor or teacher: "I understand the assignment, but I wonder if you'd allow me to turn it in a different direction, from something routine to something special."

I remember approaching my high school English teacher John Kane with an unconventional idea in response to his assignment on poems from the Enlightenment to the Romantic period: "I'd like to write an essay about eighteenth-century English poetry in poetic form, using rhyming couplets — the way Alexander Pope did in his satiric essays." John Kane gave me a skeptical look. "I promise it will be as long or longer than five hundred words. I'm not taking a shortcut." In his wisdom, he said, "Show me a sample — tomorrow." When he read about ten lines, he was sold. I could indeed make the assignment my own. He wound up reading it to the class. Even better, one of my friends came up later to tell me how cool he thought it was.

This strategy has carried over into my professional work. I had the opportunity to do a telephone interview with horror author Stephen King. (It was so early in his career that he had not yet made his first million dollars!) In preparation, I had read *Carrie* and *Salem's Lot* and *The Shining*. I knew how many of these marketing interviews he would be giving and did not want to become a channel for a set of automatic answers. I persuaded my editor to try something different: I wrote a scene that was meant to imitate King's style. Although the scene of his speaking to me through the flames of a creepy fireplace was obviously invented, his quotes garnered from the interview were real.

Your goal is not to sneak around your teacher or editor. It's to turn that person into an ally, not an adversary. Surprises may delight an ordinary reader, but not a teacher or an editor, who will expect the final work to adhere to directions. So by all means try something new. But first send up a flare.

Take what you think is a bad assignment and brainstorm with other writers on how to turn it into something special.

Get an assignment about the features of the new phone book? Feel the power of the collective: "You could write it as a book review." "Call any number at random and write a story about that person." "Look up the first name in the phone book." "Look up the last name." "I thought they were going to do away with White Pages."

This technique is not unlike jazz improvisation. Someone begins with an idea, and others pick up on it as if it were a musical riff. It might emerge as something like this:

"I've been assigned to write about the time change."

"You mean like: Don't forget to turn your clocks back this Sunday?"

"Yeah, just like that. What more is there to say?"

"Interview Benjamin Franklin."

"Excuse me?"

"Yeah, old Ben invented the idea of daylight saving time."

"Who is most affected by the time change?"

"Maybe people who get up early on Sunday to go to church?"

"Who else?"

"Animals can't tell time. Maybe the dogs in the kennels get out of sorts when their food arrives too early or too late."

This is not just a two-player game. A group of three or more can accelerate the brainstorming process and help you build the best possible story idea out of what you thought was a dry assignment.

Talk over the story idea with some of the stakeholders or even with some friends who are not writers or editors.

It's one thing to brainstorm with other writers, and quite another to find and interview the stakeholders, those who are most influenced or affected by your topic. Perhaps you are not so eager to write a back-to-school profile of the school crossing guard. Take a cleansing breath. Then begin talking to people about school crossing guards in general. You'll find that most people have a story to tell—for better or worse —about the lady who held up her hand to stop the traffic and led little kids across the road to get to the other side.

I still remember when my elementary school hired a guard—too late to save a second-grade boy running across a busy intersection. In the seventh grade I was assigned to the safety patrol, but I was kicked off when I abandoned my post to talk to some of the cute girls getting off the school bus.

You probably got your "bad" assignment because someone, however selfishly, really cared about a news item, issue, or problem behind the assignment. So they are going to put in a speed bump on 66th Avenue South. Who cares? Well, the folks on my street, 63rd Avenue South, care because now all the speeders will come to prefer our street, unimpeded by humps or bumps. If you were assigned to this topic, you would search for me, and I would introduce you to my neighbors, the real stakeholders.

Use your favorite search engine to discover surprising connections.

In .56 of a second, more than forty thousand links become available to you for a topic such as "School Crossing Guards." A quick survey of the first twenty links reveals a variety of angles for a back-to-school story, from safety guidelines to budget problems to awards and appreciations to relationships with police departments to acts of bravery. Search engines can make writers lazy, but the aces know how to use them as starting points to identify sources, subjects, and news items so that they can better use time in the field.

Now I'll search for "speed bumps": almost six hundred thousand links. The first one includes information about conventional and unconventional speed bumps. A Wikipedia entry offers several synonyms for the term and informs us that the earliest known speed bump, as reported in the *New York Times* on June 7, 1906, was in Chatham, New Jersey. To slow traffic, the city leaders had decided to raise the pavement by five inches at dangerous crosswalks. A less predictable result is the use of "speed bump" as a political metaphor, signifying the loss of liberty when the government becomes overprotective or controlling. I am beginning to see the outlines of an interesting story on speed bumps, one that would offer readers some surprising turns along the way.

If the story assignment points left, don't be afraid to turn right.

Part of your rebellion against assignments involves a skeptical, contrarian attitude that can serve the writer and the reader well. Too often an assignment "begs the question," a technical term in logic that means the conclusion is assumed or even pre-determined in the assignment. "Go out and see why Catholic priests are more prone to abuse children than Protestant ministers or rabbis are." It is the duty of the writer to challenge the premise, which, if it is wrong, deserves debunking. Shattering a common premise makes one hell of a story.

Back in the 1980s, many parents had their young children photographed and fingerprinted in the fear that they were vulnerable to kidnapping by strangers. (Remember those scary photos on milk cartons of lost kids?) The *Denver Post* won a Pulitzer Prize by looking at the cases of missing children and discovering that although kids *were* being snatched, the snatchers were most often not strangers but noncustodial parents or their minions.

If you read a story that says young people are not going to church as much as they did thirty years ago, wait a while and then test the thesis against the available evidence. You may find it to be true. Or you might discover that the findings reflect some unintended bias of the author, or a broad generalization from a very limited body of evidence. They zig. You zag. They flim. You flam. They whiz. You bang.

At least on occasion, stop grumbling and just follow the assignment.

If you want your teacher or editor to have your back, you must have that person's back back. One way you win the privilege of working on your own story is to be a trouper rather than a prima donna or a prima dog. An assignment often comes down to you from your boss's boss with lots of fingerprints all over it. Spend as much time as you need on the story to get it done at decent quality so you can get on to more interesting work.

How much effort you give can be a tricky equation. Even some Hall of Fame football players talk about how they "took a few plays off" during a game to preserve their energy and strength for a bigger moment. This is not a fashionable option in an age when we are told to reach for the impossible "110 percent." As an editor, I would be happy with the occasional C+ performance if we were working under pressure of deadline and you, young writer, stepped in to save my ass, as they say in the newsroom.

I love the idea of the *trouper,* a word derived from show business. I used to misspell it *trooper,* as if it were a military metaphor used to describe a good soldier. Spelled *trouper,* it is defined by *The American Heritage Dictionary* as "a member of a theatrical company" and by extension "a reliable, uncomplaining, often hard-working person."

My daughter Lauren performed in a community theater production of *Sweet Charity* and was disappointed at first when she didn't get a larger role than that of one of the dance hall girls. The second lead was injured in an automobile accident, and Lauren was asked to step in just a day or two before opening night. It was too late to get another dancer, so Lauren had to play both roles. A real trouper.

Keep at hand a list of story ideas so that when you get a "bad" assignment you can try to trade it for one of yours.

"I need someone to check out this zoning variance at city hall. You up for it?"

"I'll take it if you need me to, chief, but I just started working on this tattoo story."

"Tattoo story?"

"Yeah. There's this bridge club of old ladies, and at one of their meetings they got a little tipsy and all decided to get matching tattoos."

"Yikes. What were they of?"

"Scorpions."

In such a scenario, you are sure to get to do the more interesting story. Having more story ideas than you can execute is no waste of effort. On the contrary, the exploration of ideas keeps your senses sharp, attuned to what is going down in your community and why it matters.

Out of your list, you will be able to pick the most interesting idea, or the timeliest, or the one with the most impact, or the one that matters most. Such choices are at the heart of what is called critical thinking or literary judgment, and the more story ideas you accumulate, the more defined your writing muscles will become.

3

—•—

I have trouble doing all the research.

Research until you begin to hear a repetition of stories or key information.

Such repetition is a good thing. It will strengthen your evidence and serve as a signal that it's time to move to the next stage. You will experience repetition throughout the research or reporting, and much of it will be the equivalent of background noise, a result of everyone spouting the company line or offering the most superficial conventional wisdom. Instead, you are looking for nuggets.

Let's say, for example, that you are writing a story about an influential school for journalists that began in a storefront with a tiny budget. Everyone you interview offers a different version of the same story: "It's amazing how far we've come." Or "No one could have walked into that old broken-down building and imagined we'd become a world-class institution."

Then you interview me, the only remaining person to have taught in that building. "That converted old bank building was a pit. We had termites eating our library books. And we had pigeons roosting in the ceilings." OK, termites and pigeons are good. Those are the kinds of details you're looking for. "The space was so confining that we conducted small-group work in this antique bank vault that came with the building."

More reporting will fill out these anecdotes. When you begin to hear the same key stuff from different sources, it may be the sign you need to gear down the research so that the drafting can be revved up. Most important, never use the need for more research as an excuse for not writing.

Work until you get to the unofficial experts.

Never be satisfied with official sources, human or documentary. Get deeper. Find the sources who are closest to the action. You want the investigating detective, not the public-information officer. You want the short-order cook or the waitress who takes your order without writing it down and remembers your name from a year ago. You don't want the hospital administrator; you want the neonatal nurse, the one who sews beautiful white baptismal gowns for babies who have little or no chance of surviving. Donald Murray advised writers to look not to the foreman but to the young mechanic in the shop whom everyone seems to turn to.

I remember well my opportunity to interview glamorous movie star and famous Charlie's Angel Farrah Fawcett, at the time one of the world's most recognizable celebrities. I was among a dozen reporters covering her first full-length movie, *Sunburn,* and we were being herded around so the publicity apparatus could keep us under control. While other writers were being fed pabulum, I broke away. I wasn't about to knock on her hotel room door, but I had one burning question in my mind: How do you get a celebrity like this through the Atlanta airport, into the city, through the hotel lobby, into a glass elevator, and way up to her room in the Hyatt without starting a riot? None of the publicity agents knew, but guess what? A member of the hotel staff was in charge of such squiring. She knew the ropes and was flattered that I asked her to show them to me.

Ask yourself if you have enough evidence to support a powerful conclusion.

If you research long enough, you will experience a dominant feeling or reach a strong conclusion. When you can re-create the evidence that led you there, you probably have enough. There is quite a distance between "feeling" and "concluding," the former an expression of an emotion, the latter a destination reached through logic and reason.

Here is a feeling I remember from years ago: "I wish my daughters would stop hooking up with all these nice-looking slacker boys and find caring and responsible men for friendship and marriage."

Here is a conclusion: "Based on an examination of the graduation rates by gender, there is a growing gap between the academic performance of boys and girls, men and women. The women are leaving the men in the dust."

Here is evidence: "If my alma mater, which was once an all-male school, accepted students by academic merit alone, the school would have a female enrollment above 60 percent."

As you gather evidence from many different kinds of sources, pay close attention to what that evidence tells you—especially how it makes you feel. As that feeling grows into a conclusion, you can move the dial from the collecting stage to finding a focus, or even drafting.

Report until you begin to see more and more stuff that you can leave out.

It may help you to see your work in the form of a funnel. The top of the funnel is wide. That's where you pour in everything you've gathered for the story. But as the shape of the funnel narrows to a spout, the writer must become more selective, reaching a point where he can leave things out with confidence.

In an interview with the *Paris Review*, Nobel laureate Elie Wiesel described the tension between aggregation and curation, that is, adding stuff up as opposed to taking stuff out:

> Writing is not like painting, where you add. It is not what you put on the canvas that the reader sees. Writing is more like a sculpture, where you remove, you eliminate in order to make the work visible. Even those pages you remove somehow remain. There is a difference between a book of two hundred pages from the very beginning, and a book of two hundred pages which is the result of an original eight hundred pages. The six hundred pages are there. Only you don't see them.

As we will see down the road, you will make sharper choices if you come to understand what your story is really about. That magnifying glass will help you concentrate the light and burn out the weeds. Look for those moments when you can articulate with complete confidence what your story is about. Sometimes it's a single fact discovered in mounds of research that delivers a working theme, one that can help in the gathering of information and eventually in the selection of details.

Research until you have heard someone say: "You've got to talk to Shirley." And then talk to Shirley.

We've all met Shirley, who can be old or young, rich or poor, male or female. My mother's name happens to be Shirley, and if you are writing a history of Italian Americans who migrated from Italy to the Lower East Side of Manhattan, you must talk to her. Shirley is ninety-two. Her memory is sharp, her reflections spicy, and when it comes to talking, God bless her, she is relentless, indefatigable. You can ask her:

- What kind of street games did the Italian kids play back then?
- Did people really pin money to religious statues during festivals of saints?
- What did you eat during the Depression years? Did you ever feel hungry and unable to do anything about it?
- Is it true that a famous gangster was shot and died in your grandmother's arms?
- I've watched the movie *The Godfather* about fifty times. I'm always fascinated by the wedding scene. Tell me what you remember about Italian American weddings.

A Shirley can verify notions you've heard elsewhere and provide evidence available nowhere else. A Shirley can help you decide if your reporting is done. But don't be surprised if you hear a Shirley say, "You can't do this story until you've talked to Tony." That may require a good bit of hanging around, watching the official experts as they turn to the shop veteran who then turns to the unofficial expert always closest to the action: Tony.

Get busy writing *before* *your editor or teacher starts* *yelling at you because you're about to miss a deadline.*

The most significant part of the word *deadline* is not "line," but "dead." In fact, there is a language of death that governs and distorts our thinking about the craft of writing. Old newspaper stories, for example, were kept in a "morgue." Editors "spiked" stories, or "cut" them, or "buried" them. Famous writers talked about "sweating blood" during the process, or "opening a vein." Even though these are dysphemisms—negative exaggerations— they reveal the trepidation that infects the craft, even at the highest level.

I too struggle as a writer. I have perfectionist tendencies. Not long ago, they made me miss an important book deadline. I have learned the hard way that struggle and delay are not virtues or signs of greatness. Nor, in most cases, are they necessary.

Do everything in your power to meet your deadlines, and that often requires handing in work that is not as good as you hoped it would be. If you are a student, you may need to make a cold calculation: Handing in B work on time is better than handing in A work a week late. That missed deadline may turn your A into a C.

It is more complicated for professionals. Someone who misses deadlines with regularity may risk losing a job. Even if that is not the case, a deadline crasher makes work harder for everyone else on the team. The editor lacks time to work with the writer on improving the story. The photo editor and page designer lack the time to do their best work.

Writers often devote a disproportionate amount of their time to research, leaving writing to the very end. I know writers who researched a story for ten months and gave themselves only ten hours to draft it. So when you hear the bell tower chime the hour, it's a reliable sign that you should begin drafting. Your story will not be perfect, but most times "good enough" is good enough. Feel the adrenaline. Use it. Then let the work go.

Work until you can write a clear statement of what the story is really about.

This statement can take many forms: a note to yourself, a memo to the editor, a tentative lead sentence or paragraph, a theme statement. To write an effective version of any of these requires a knowledge that derives from your research. It's evidence enough that even the first draft of your story will have a clear focus.

Pitch a story to a helper:

Dear Lindsay: Here's an idea I have for an essay titled "Me and My Shadow." I've borrowed that title from a popular song from the 1930s; it fits my analysis of one of my favorite nursery poems: "My Shadow," by Robert Louis Stevenson. That poem describes a little boy who grows weary and impatient with his unruly shadow, which seems to take on a life of its own in the span of a simple day. I've just discovered that Stevenson wrote this poem about the same time he wrote *Dr. Jekyll and Mr. Hyde,* a story whose very title has become an archetype for the good side and the shadowy side of human nature. I read this poem as a child; the language in the poem has not changed, but I have changed. My adult perspective, perhaps too cynical for my own good, sees through the bright surface of the poem to find something dark lurking beneath.

My ability to write that memo, and draw those conclusions, indicates to me that I have enough to fire up a full draft.

Research until you have enough to show the reader — not just tell the reader.

It is easier to *tell* someone something important about your story than to *show* the reader. For that you need strong evidence drawn from your research. Consider the work of Anne Hull and Dana Priest, reporters from the *Washington Post,* who exposed that Walter Reed Army Medical Center was providing substandard care to wounded veterans returning home from war in the Middle East.

Hull slept on the floor of hospital rooms, essentially living with soldiers and spouses during the difficult process of physical and psychological rehabilitation. As a result of this immersion, she was able to describe scenes such as this one:

When the 20-year-old infantry soldier woke up, he was on the locked-down psychiatric ward at Walter Reed Army

Medical Center. A nurse handed him pajamas and a robe, but they reminded him of the flowing clothes worn by Iraqi men. He told the nurse, "I don't want to look like a freakin' Haj." He wanted his uniform. Request denied. Shoelaces and belts were prohibited.

When a writer has achieved that level of scenic detail — the ability to open up a world that the reader can enter — she can proceed to the drafting of the story with confidence.

Hunt and gather until you have three times as much as you think you need.

Good writers collect much more than they need, but that's not what makes them good. What makes them good is an ability to select the best material from all they have gathered. It's a bit like harvesting fruit. Some years the citrus tree in our backyard produces as few as twenty or thirty decent tangerines. Other years, the crop is ten times those numbers. The more fruit on the tree, the more selective we can be as we harvest them for our breakfasts or for friends.

With the exception of short texts written on tight deadline, the author wants to gather at least twice as much as is needed for the final work. In other words, the writer needs the so-so stuff in order to recognize what the best stuff looks like. It is not uncommon for writers to gather more than ten times the amount they need for a story. That may be required for certain investigations, but in general you will ease off on your research at the point where you begin to recognize that you have way more than enough.

This problem of selection is as real for the novelist as it is for the journalist. In the collection of his letters *Editor to Author,* Scribner's editor Maxwell Perkins can be found, time and again, encouraging writers to select their details according to the focus of the story. "All this is based on the assumption," wrote Perkins to Canadian novelist Morley Callaghan, "that when one writes a story he does not...put everything in, but selects with a view to the motive of the story." He then chides Callaghan for not being selective enough.

The ability to select wisely comes with experience. I believe, for example, that I am now a better teacher than ever; and yet I do much less preparation for any particular class. It's not because it's easy for me to recycle earlier lessons; it's because I have a much better sense of how much material is necessary to create a good hour or ninety minutes of learning.

New teachers almost always bring ten suitcases to the curb when the trunk of the car can fit only five. "I did not know how I could even fill the time for a fifty-five-minute class," one new teacher told me. "And suddenly the class was over and I didn't get to more than half of my material."

Collect material until you have enough to recognize and select the best stuff.

As you conduct research, you will begin to imagine what the key parts of your story will be. You will recognize, for example, that nothing you learned in that hour interview with the school principal will wind up in the story. In no way does that make that hour useless. The writer needs to hear many voices. Some will be quoted loud and clear, helping the reader to understand what the story is about. Others provide the writer with important background information, which can be used now or stored for future work. Other voices are not so strong: confused, inarticulate, careless, scattered. But it may take hearing those weaker voices for the writer to recognize the stronger ones.

So what makes some story material "good" or even "the best"? Apply these tests:

Is it interesting? That is, does it capture your attention as a writer? If not, it will be hard to make it interesting to the reader. When something is interesting, we are eager to share it with others. "Hey, Karen, did you read the story today about the people who were stuck upside down on the roller coaster?" "How did they get them down?" "I don't know. I haven't gotten to that part yet."

Is it important? There may be unhealthy traces of lead in drywall imported from China. Do not, repeat do not, try to sneak your pets into the hurricane shelter. Some gun proponents want to arm schoolteachers. Each of these statements has important implications for individual readers, families, and the community at large.

Does it support the focus of the story? This happens all the time: You research a story about the danger of fireworks, especially to young children. Along the way, you discover an eighty-year-old man from Italy who has designed and executed thousands of fireworks displays without a single injury to himself or his crew. Now you find that most interesting. You like the detail enough that you may get out the old shoehorn and wedge it into the story somewhere. It takes discipline to leave it out, but leave it out you must. Your story is not about old Italian men who have not been injured by fireworks; it's about children who have. Now, if that old man is missing a finger from a cherry bomb explosion when he was a child...

—•—

Getting Your Act Together

No writer writes well from thin air—or a chair. The productive writer is a tracker, collecting data, information from interviews, online research, narrative elements such as scenes and dialogue, memories and personal observations, and key words and interesting language.

To accomplish this part well, the writer must spend time and energy getting organized; as one student put it so aptly: "getting your shit together." Minutes spent here will save hours down the line for writers who must find *what* they need *when* they need it. More savvy (and geeky) scribes will make use of the benefits that come with sophisticated word processing, search engines, social networks, and computer files, all managed electronically. Most writers, even young ones, will make use of at least some old-school strategies for physical organization. For me, this involves cardboard file boxes, a rolling set of hanging files, reference books, index cards, manuscript boxes to hold multiple drafts, and a moderately uncluttered and well-lit writing space.

I need an organized workplace because I am about to launch into hours, days, months, years of research on a particular project. I will be scouring the landscape for the raw materials I need to make the work good, everything from character details, to anecdotes, to unusual and compelling facts, to words spoken in wisdom or anger, to sequences of scenes, to ideas that support or challenge the status quo. I will gather much more than I can use in a story. The material left aside is not wasted. Like the house foundation in the ground, it may not be visible, but it holds up and supports the roof beams.

Problems covered in this chapter:

SO DISORGANIZED

Enter the office or workplace of some writers and you find yourself in the space of a crazed hoarder, with years' worth of newspapers stacked up, files on the floor, last week's Styrofoam cups filled with cigarette ashes. No wonder they can't get their arms around the story. Before a writer can plan a story, that writer must organize the material: cleaning, stacking, collating, compiling, tossing, filing, and indexing. The bigger the meal to be served, the more carefully the table must be set.

Remember, though, that the compulsive person can be a cleaner or a hoarder. Work spaces can be immaculate or rat infested—two different effects, both the product of an obsessive-compulsive personality. If I can extend that distinction to writers, I have met both kinds: the ones whose desks must be free of clutter every day, and the ones whose offices have been marked as fire hazards (not kidding).

If the range from cleaner to hoarder is, say, one to ten, then a healthy writer can live and work productively and happily between four and seven. Too much neatness may be the sign of an uncurious mind, too much clutter the sign of an undisciplined mind. If you are both uncurious and undisciplined, I'd love to have a photo of your office.

JUST CAN'T FIND IT

An author with the wonderful name Mihaly Csikszentmihalyi (his friends call him Mike) wrote a book titled *Flow: The Psychology of Optimal Experience*. In it, he argues that when we are at our best—in work or play—things, even hard things, seem to flow, keeping us oblivious to the difficulty of the task or the time it takes to carry it out. Writers sometimes have this feeling—that everything you read, see, or discuss reflects on the work that now surrounds you. Some writers say, "The story just wrote itself." In other words: flow.

Tidy and efficient work habits make flow possible. Clutter and disorganization become blood clots in the body of work. While it is no disaster having to spend an afternoon looking for that missing file or that elusive fact (you will be rehearsing your story while you search), it is not the ideal condition.

The ideal is to be able to find exactly what you need when you need it. That means putting books on your shelf in some meaningful order. It means having clear labels on files. It means cross-referencing and collating your notes. For author John Capouya it means coding the material in different colors.

TOO MUCH STUFF

A common complaint of writers working on big projects is "I just could not get my arms around the material." I think of this as tree hugging. Children sometimes measure the size of a tree—and their own wingspans—by putting their arms around it.

The phrase "too much material" is relative to the scope of your project, the time you have to work on it, and your mission and purpose. If you have lots of time to sort through research material, then there can never be "too much." If you have a tough deadline to meet, you may have to limit the scope of the idea from the beginning and then hunt and gather with a sharp focus in mind.

A tough sticking point is often less of a problem in itself than a manifestation of missteps earlier in the process. So don't be afraid to call a time-out and take a step or two back and try again.

REFLECT

- Which parts of research do you find tedious or intimidating?
- What forms of research most interest you?
- Can you think of a piece of writing that is very well researched? What effect does that research have on you as a reader?

- What would people who didn't know you say about your desk, office, or work space?
- During the writing process, do you find it easy or hard to find what you need when you need it?
- Do you consider yourself organized or disorganized?
- Interview a writer who has her "shit together" and record what you learn.

4

—•—

My work habits are so disorganized.

*Clean out the clutter in your writing space. Stash or
hide anything you can't use on your current project.*

You need a dedicated work space for each writing project. It's
worth the time to do some spring cleaning because too much
messiness wastes time and saps energy. Just this morning, I saw a
Twitter feed from famed nonfiction author Susan Orlean: "Boy,"
she wrote, "if I didn't have a book project, I would never get my
closets organized."

But wait. Shouldn't she be writing instead of cleaning her
closets? Maybe she's doing both at the same time. Or maybe
she needs to clean closets in order to clear out the cobwebs in
her mind that inhibit writing. In other words, Grasshopper, she
may need to "not write" in order to "write."

Signs of the imminent birth of a child include a "nesting

impulse" on the part of the mother. A pregnant woman dusting, vacuuming, storing, painting walls, and stacking baby clothes is like a mother osprey in Florida grabbing a clutch of pine needles in her talons and flying them to the top of a light stand in a supermarket parking lot.

To the extent that the delivery of a manuscript or work assignment is akin, metaphorically, to the birth of a baby, it should not surprise us that the beginning of a writing process would reveal a whole lotta nestin' goin' on. Like Orlean, I often direct my cleaning efforts at spaces and things — the garage, my golf clubs — not directly related to the writing project. But cleaning out that pile of junk in the corner of my office provides me with a kind of training for the more direct job of organizing my writing materials.

Index and date your notebooks and place them on a shelf according to project and in chronological order.

Writing teacher Donald Murray was the consummate planner. He was famous for capturing his thoughts and organizing his time through a daybook. Before his death, Murray donated his literary effects to the Poynter Institute, and it has been a remarkable learning process to immerse myself in this material, experiencing the long arc of a writing life but also explosive little moments of discovery. If you were to go through the Murray collection, you would be struck by the sequence of daybooks, close to a hundred of them, lined up in chronological order.

For the record, Murray preferred the National Brand Narrow Ruled Eye-Ease Paper 1 Subject Notebook, Reorder # 33008, 80 Sheets, 10" × 8", distributed by Rediform Inc., out of

Coppell, TX, 75019. I've included those facts in homage to Murray's attention to detail. He was ready, in ways that I am not, to record and process and index and annotate and compile, willing to do the roll-up-your-sleeves scut work as a foundation upon which to build a beautiful cathedral. So, do you want to be a person, like me, who keeps all his nails, nuts, and screws in a coffee can and dumps them out when looking for a ¾-inch whatever? Or would you prefer to be like my friend Don Fry, whose garage looks like a world-class operating room, with little plastic containers—labeled, of course—to hold all his different geegaws? Let me put it this way: If I need something in a hurry, I'd prefer to search for it in Don's garage, not mine.

If your project has an obvious beginning, middle, and end, divide your working materials into those categories.

If you are not a sophisticated organizer, I encourage you to try the Three-Box Solution. Three is a powerful number because it communicates a sense of the whole. It encompasses everything. That's why the number three, at least in literature, is higher than four. Higher than any other number. If I show you three examples of well-organized writers, it feels as if I were giving you every such writer who exists.

Carry this into writing, and the number three can stand for both the structure of a story and the process you use to create it. Every piece of writing, even a haiku, has a beginning, a middle, and an ending. Even a story with a five-part structure—one of Shakespeare's plays, for example—is a three-part structure in disguise. That's because the middle part often is divided into three key elements. You can't escape it. *Three* is the word.

So embrace it. Get yourself three boxes. Mark one

"Beginning," the next one "Middle," the last one "End." Sort through your notes, clippings, and source materials with these boxes in mind. If you come across an anecdote that summarizes the points you want to make, perhaps it belongs in the "End" box. A startling statistic may go near the beginning. A quote that offers good evidence or testimony might go in the middle. You can always move things from box to box, leave some material out, or put something aside till it becomes clearer where it should go.

In your journal or daybook, write down your mission for that day's work.

Let's call this the "day mission," rather than a larger statement of purpose that describes why you are working on a project. A day mission asks, simply, "What would I like to accomplish today?"

Here's mine for today, 4/26/10: "I have to work on three or four different writing tasks today. If I can make a little progress on each, it will have been a productive day. I want to write four solutions for writers who need *Help!* I need to make a reading copy of my grammar book so I can begin audio recordings. I need to gather the books I'll need to research my preface to a book on journalism and realism."

When I make such a list, I have to prepare myself for the eventuality, if not inevitability, that I will not complete my day mission. As my mother, Shirley, likes to say, "Tomorrow's always another day." Whatever you don't get done today can become a part of the next day's mission. Self-forgiveness is a crucial virtue for the happy and productive writer.

What's the difference between "daily goals" and "day

mission"? Not much, probably, but I'm influenced by the differences in word origin. The word *goal* comes to us from Old English, where it meant "barrier," and Middle English, where it meant "boundary." It suggests something to hurdle. *Mission,* on the other hand, comes from the Latin verb "to send." I like that better. I am sent to accomplish something important; I'm a missionary of the word.

Under your day mission, list the tasks necessary to complete it.

Where does the writing rubber meet the road? Maybe it's the spot when you realize you must accomplish a specific, finite list of tasks in order to fulfill your mission. So, returning to the previous example from my own work, I would list these little labors necessary to begin the audio version of my grammar book:

- Reread the specs and check them with Jeff to make sure we have all the sound equipment we need.
- Call Paul at the audio publishers and ask him about his expectations and his company's protocols.
- Send an electronic file to Sir Speedy printers so that I can have a reading manuscript that I can rehearse and mark up.

I've already accomplished those tasks (it's now 2:26 p.m.) and am waiting to find out when I'll be able to get my hands on the manuscript.

In the meantime, I am working on *Help! For Writers* and, given the time of day, will wait until I get home to look through my book collection for helpful texts on realism. Maybe I'll watch a couple of reality shows to see if they might be relevant for my argument.

A mission statement of any kind must be expressed in strategies and tactics. It cannot be frozen in time. It will change. Expect it to melt and flow into something else.

Place your tasks in a practical and meaningful order.

Some writers perform the easiest task first to get a running start on the day. That often works for me. I can liberate myself from the inertia of morning and get things rolling. I have to be careful, though, because it can also serve as a form of delay for the larger, more important, more arduous chores ahead.

When you come down to it, the world of work, including writing, is most influenced by two powerful forces: (1) How will I make use of my time? (2) Among the things I'm working on, what matters most? Often it is time that dominates: How much of this project can I complete in the time allotted? And sometimes priority holds sway: Is this important enough to spend an extra day getting it just right?

So it's not enough to have a list of tasks. You can't complete everything on the list until you complete one thing on the list. Which one will that be? Your decisions do not petrify. If you choose to plan interview questions for the graffiti artist and you hit a wall, jump to another item on your list. Remember: The list serves you; you are not slave to the list.

Cross out the tasks as you finish them.

Nothing satisfies a writer more than completing an important task—unless it's cashing an advance check. When this book is published, I'm sure we'll spend a little moolah on a small celebration with family and friends. Book publication parties recognize all the work, physical and intellectual, that marks the end of a creative labor that can take years.

But please don't wait until the end of a project to celebrate. You need more moments of joy than that, rewards that are scattered across the span of a writing project like gorgeous shells on a long sandy beach. Look for opportunities to mark off significant accomplishments: when you've drafted and revised a book or project proposal, landed a contract, met the deadline for a first draft, completed a significant revision, responded to a set of inquiries from copy editors, read the page proofs, and much more.

You can't expect a party (with a cake!) for the completion of each task, but at least give yourself credit for mastering a particular challenge. At the very least, gain the satisfaction of crossing a task off your to-do list.

What applies to book-length projects also works on a smaller scale. I plan to write a short essay juxtaposing two events that occurred in Tucson, Arizona, in 2011. In January, a crazed gunman shot and killed six people, including a young girl, at a small political gathering in a shopping plaza. U.S. Representative Gabrielle Giffords was shot in the head, and she continues to recover from her injuries. Two months later more than a hundred thousand folks convened for the Tucson Festival of Books, one of the nation's largest celebrations of literacy. As a guest author, I felt inspired by the ways a devastated community tried to heal from its wounds, declaring to the world that books can be mightier than bullets.

Writing this essay requires the completion of some obvious tasks, and here is my first draft of a list:

- Review stories about the Tucson shootings to harvest the most important facts.
- Do some reporting to find out the current status of victims and families.
- Interview a newspaper publisher on how the festival helped bring the community together for a positive cause.
- Interview Frank Deford, who was a main speaker, and Elmore Leonard, who was honored.
- Spend some time capturing details of Arizona culture that mark it as wild and dangerous: deserts, cacti, guns, snakes, tarantulas, scorpions, the OK Corral.
- Identify as many people as possible who were involved in the aftermath of the shootings and who also attended the reading festival.

By the time I've written my essay, this list of tasks will grow and shrink and grow some more as my scattered thousand words begin to take shape. Chances are, I will pin my task list above my desk. As I complete each task, I may not break out the caviar and champagne, but I can assure you of this: I will cross it off my list—with flair.

Leave one task for the next day.

I doubt it's possible to transform from a compulsive hoarder to a compulsive cleaner, even though both may share some deep-seated neuroses. If you were a new worker here at Poynter, I could have fun giving you a tour of two offices, each one representative of a certain worker mentality. Office A can only be described as belonging to a semi-hoarder. Books and newspapers are stacked everywhere. No sign of the desktop. To get to it, you'd have to clear away papers, pens, office supplies, knickknacks, empty water bottles, the odd food fossil (my favorite is the paleolithic french fry), and much else.

Then I'll take you to office B. Here sits a woman who cannot bear to leave the day's work until it's completed, finished. A bare, squeaky-clean desktop is the sign of another happy and productive day.

As usual, I represent some middle path. I am neither hoarder nor cleaner. I'm a "cloarder." I do not want to leave the office with a pristine desktop. If I faced a clean desk in the morning, it would be hard for me to get started. This is why I will leave on my desk a token of one thing I want to do the next day. It may simply be a book I'll want to consult. Or a name and phone number I need to call. Uncluttered works for me. Empty and bare do not.

Keep files or boxes in which you "save string" for future projects.

Saving string is an old-school idea that still works. There is a kind of Franklinian economy in the adage "Waste not, want not." The little piece of string may not be useful right now, but what if it became the core of a planet of string? The key is that you are never conscious of the work it takes to add new string. Before you know it, you can wind electrical tape around it and use it as a baseball.

It helps me immensely to have a physical place where I can store my string. That photo I took of the new Italian restaurant is a piece of string that goes in a file. Then I find a magazine article about the history of pizza. My mother sends me her oldest recipe for an Italian dish. Each of these goes into a box marked "The Story of Italian Americans." Before long, I realize that I've got a lot of stuff in this box, even a handful of files with materials about particular Italian Americans: Sinatra, DiMaggio, La Guardia.

By having a place to save your string, you accomplish two tasks. You grow a new topic for study and writing, and you give your raw materials a chance to breathe. They are not mixed in with the rest of your crapola. They grow and grow over time into something significant, something that eventually calls your name to start writing.

Save the tools you have used to organize your best work.

Athletes, we know, are not always at their best; they fall into slumps, suffer injuries, and discover limitations imposed by aging. Coaches who work with athletes have a tested tool for grading and improving performance. They study videos from the past, especially when the athletes were at their best, in hopes that the runner, swimmer, or boxer can regain that championship form.

Writers are athletes of the imagination (or, in my case, *in* my imagination). When you feel a slump coming on, it will help you to read examples of your best work and to re-create the elements of craft that produced it, especially the tools of organization. These can be dusted off, sharpened, and put into action time and again.

I always feel the need to throw away the redundant materials that grow out of a writing project. No need, for example, to keep nine paper versions of a manuscript when each of them has been preserved in electronic files. The physical act of cleaning out my space is a symbol of clearing my mind for my next project.

I like to save and store the most important pieces of a finished product, especially if they don't take up much physical space. I save, for example, the spiral notebooks that contain the earliest plans for a book and my first efforts at turning ideas into language. I save index cards that helped me capture the discrete parts or chapters, the puzzle pieces that were once tacked to my bulletin board so that I could see the whole and move bits around. I also transfer my hanging files from a rolling cart to a single file box, which I can place in a corner or store in a closet.

I use these tools to demonstrate my methods to other writers. I also need them to remind me that the best work takes time and a set of reliable tactics and routines that can serve the productive writer throughout a lifetime of labor and delivery.

5

—•—

I can never find what I need when I need it.

Set up an organizational plan as early as possible.

Some writers organize their bookshelves alphabetically by author, others by subject matter, and others—including at least one person I know—by a combination of size and color. I'm not very good at this, which is why I often discover that I've purchased two or three copies of the same book. I'm not bragging. My random storage slows me down, so I'm working on a new system, an organizational plan in which the books I need are displayed on a more prominent shelf, with other, distracting volumes cleared out of sight.

The bigger the project, the more detailed the plan. No other equation works, especially for the writer who is disorganized by disposition. If you don't know how to draft a plan, ask for some advice, as if you were bringing in a professional to help you organize your closets. After all, a closet usually contains a certain number of classifiable objects: shirts, slacks, dresses, robes, shoes, sweaters, suits, and maybe some odds and ends placed on a convenient shelf. Most people would feel organized if they at least put the items together that belong together. It's easier to find a shirt if it's with the other shirts rather than hung at random. In the same way, your raw material contains notes, books, clippings, research, photographs, etc.

Your subject area, no matter how focused, has parts. Make a list of the parts of your story and name those parts: baseball in Florida, domed stadiums, rough summer weather, retirees with limited incomes. Those topics can easily become the names for some of your most important files.

Make copies of your most important research materials.

This strategy will not waste time or paper. Most writers come to know so much through their research that they do not even know what they know. So this review of your materials requires you to make decisions about what is essential and what is marginal. You can always retrieve that odd element from the corner, but you are now forced to discriminate. The act of copying in this context is an act of learning. I've seen some writers actually retype their notes so that the sorting and selecting process can begin in earnest.

The process of copying can proceed digitally or analogically. The value of doing it the old-school way is that it takes more time, and that time can be used to organize your best research into the appropriate piles. That distribution can be done in relation to the subtopics of your main theme or it can be congruent with the structure of your story, perhaps using piles marked beginning, middle, and end.

Surround yourself with your most important references.

I disliked my high school junior varsity basketball coach. And Old Joe did not like me. After a game in which I played poorly, he told me I needed a haircut (good coaching, Joe). Some games I started, some I entered as an early substitute, and a few I sat out on the the bench. If I was out of favor I sat down where he couldn't see me. When things were better, he sat me next to him so that I could hear his commentary on the game and prepare to play.

That strategy applies to writing projects. I keep my favorite or most important reference works near at hand. These begin with my dictionaries: *The American Heritage* and the *Merriam-Webster's Collegiate* are close enough that I can lean over and grab them with my left hand. The *Oxford English Dictionary* (two-volume microprint edition) is on a convenient shelf six steps away. The plays of Shakespeare and other classic works of literature occupy a narrow four-shelf bookcase.

These are my starters, but I also have some players on the bench. When I need one or more of them, I draw them closer to my writing space, sometimes surrounding me on the rug or stacked neatly on the edge of the desk. For example, when I was writing about anti-Semitism, I kept the testimonies of Holocaust survivors nearby; when I'm writing about race in America, a collection of essays by W. E. B. DuBois stands at attention.

Work with pixels and paper.

It's been at least two decades since I first heard the claims that new information technologies would create paperless offices. So far, that prediction has not been fulfilled. In fact, the fluency of revision and the ease of printing have probably resulted in the use and abuse of more paper—"dead trees," as described by the technophiliacs in the room.

While we share environmental responsibilities, we live and work in the middle of something unprecedented, a true information revolution, perhaps greater in its consequences than the advent of the printing press or the Industrial Revolution. I typed my first book, *Free to Write,* on a Royal standard manual typewriter. Now I have more computing power in my pocket than had the space capsules that traveled to the moon. I've become an old-school-meets-new-school writer, neither Luddite nor geek. Computer files offer me clean and easy storage, rational categories of organization, and the ability to cut and paste and revise with ease.

Paper files provide more than simple backup. They help me see the whole body of work at once if I want to. They allow my hands and memory to function as a search engine parallel to the ones in my computer. If I lose my way in paper, I can always return to pixels.

Back up your files.

As someone who has lost a least a dozen unpublished stories over the years, I can testify to the need to back up your electronic files. Wherever you work or go to school, make sure you get good advice on the best ways to protect your work. It is hard to wipe out electronic files, either by accident or intent, but it does happen, so get backup from CDs and flash drives.

Secure printouts in two separate locations.

While you want all the technological support that computer science can provide, you should also consider the value of people power. Jeff Saffan, Julie Moos, Don Fry, Jane Dystel, and Tracy Behar are friends and colleagues who have become my "backup" singers, the keepers of the flame.

At various stages of the writing process, I will send one or more of these helpers a full set of computer files, essentially the piece of a project I have created so far. During the course of writing a book, I may share files for backup a half-dozen times. Jeff takes the extra step of burning a CD for me with the content so far. He writes the name of the book on the CD, as well as the date, so that it can be distinguished from other versions.

Index and cross-reference.

Part of your plan for creating backup should include some redundancy in your indexing system. In other words, you want to pilot a writing jet that has at least three engines.

As an example, I can describe a plan that evolved to organize the physical space and working materials for my book *The Glamour of Grammar*. Imagine a shelf of books, a small table stacked with the most relevant material, and, in my computer, several versions of a working draft. I created a set of hanging files, each one corresponding to a possible book chapter. I had a parallel set of index cards with possible chapter titles. Those index cards were also marked with annotations that pointed me to additional material I might need ("Don't forget to copy stuff from Orwell and Huxley"). The material in the hanging files pointed me to the early drafts of chapters stored in my computer.

So, if I needed something right away, I had three possible ways to retrieve it. Once this system was created, I could draft much more quickly because I had eliminated the energy-sapping distraction of trying to find something that I just knew was there — somewhere, but where?

Create a wall map.

An investigative team from the *St. Petersburg Times* produced a series of stories exposing the abuse of children at a school for troubled youth in north Florida. It was an ambitious and public-spirited project that helped create long-needed reforms and earned several important awards, including selection as one of three finalists for a Pulitzer Prize.

A reporter and editor who created "For Their Own Good" took me on a tour of their workspace, a small conference room on the third floor. The walls of the office were completely covered with stuff in progress: texts, photographs, timelines, key players, revealing documents. Essentially, the room provided a 360-degree view of the story, a circle of narrative.

A famous example of a wall map comes from Gay Talese, author of "Frank Sinatra Has a Cold," one of the most famous magazine profiles of the twentieth century. From his extensive reporting, research, and personal observation, Talese developed the story around a sequence of scenes. He created a series of poster-size pages, hung on the walls near his writing space. Together they formed a narrative quilt, an organic index of the evolving work. I've heard that Talese could stand back to consider the big connections between the parts, but also viewed his map through small binoculars so he could focus on the fine print.

Research it again if necessary.

It happens all the time, so do not feel embarrassed by the loss of key research material. Even if you know it's not lost, only hiding, you may not have time to track it down. When that is the case, bite the bullet, as they say, and report it again. No need to be confessional: "I'm sorry, Mayor Bigshot, but I left my notebook in my daughter's car, which I was borrowing that day, and she drove it back to college. So I'm afraid I'm going to have to ask you those questions about your marital infidelities again." Instead, just tell your source, if you are lucky enough to gain access, that you are double-checking information that you gathered earlier. "I want to make absolutely sure that I get this right" is an irresistible invitation for more conversation. Your source really wants you to be on the mark. And so do you.

Even better, the curse may turn into a blessing. Chances are, if the mayor speaks with you again, he will tell you some things that were missing from the first interview. Perhaps he has remembered something. Or perhaps he trusts your professionalism. It is common wisdom among journalists that the extra phone call or interview always helps, and that the source may be most expressive at the moment you've tucked your notebook into your back pocket.

Beware the dark side of technology.

I believe the meaning of *schadenfreude* now includes taking pleasure in the failures of technology, especially when computer geniuses like Apple's Steve Jobs or Microsoft's Bill Gates suffer through glitches during a major presentation of a new product. It's actually comforting.

But the history of communication is marked not just by the evolution of technologies such as the telegraph, radio, television, and the Internet, but also by catastrophic failures of technology. One of the most famous involves World War II photographer Robert Capa, who shipped four rolls of film from the beaches of Normandy in 1944 back to England for development. Haste to publish the images led to problems in the darkroom and to the destruction of all but eight of the grainy negatives.

Much more common are stories from frustrated researchers of sound recorders that did not work or Internet connections that failed at exactly the wrong time. There is, of course, an escape hatch. Its name is Plan B. The more important the project, the more careful and elaborate the backup plan needs to be. "If the Skype video cuts out, what can we do?" "Well, we know we'll be able to get sound even if we can't get the images."

Inventory your materials at key points in the process.

Think of your writing project as a football game, a match with four quarters. After each quarter, the teams take a short break and switch ends of the field. The announcer reviews what just happened and perhaps goes over the stats, such as yards gained or time of possession.

In the same way, you can take a little break at key intervals in your process: after the research, when you are about to select your best material, after a first draft...At such points your time-out can be used to examine your working materials, perhaps restoring or revising their order.

Ask yourself essential questions:

- What have I forgotten?
- What is still missing?
- What will I need for the next step in the process?
- What do I still have to learn?
- What could make this better?

These questions are important enough to qualify as another stage of the writing process, one I describe as "assessing your progress," to which we will devote all of Step Six.

6

—•—

I have too much material to handle.

Write for a while without reference to your notes.

Even if your notes are well organized, they can bog you down.
Give yourself time to write about what you already know. This
advice goes against the grain for those who think of the writing
process in two parts: research then writing. This book suggests
that you can be drafting or predrafting, if you prefer, all
through the process. Here are benefits of that early writing:

- It will help you learn what you already know.
- It will help you unveil that which is most memorable.
- It will suggest directions you may follow next.
- It will identify holes in your knowledge and research
  that can be filled with additional work.

- It will give you something to talk about with your writing helpers.

This strategy derives from the understanding that writing is not just a form of communication between the writer and the audience. Before that connection is made, the writer uses writing to record, to remember, to draw preliminary conclusions, to jot down the key pieces that are likely to wind up in the final draft.

Go through your notes and mark the very best material with three stars (***).

I worked with one writer who found herself engulfed in research material for her story, so I tried this technique on her. "Make a list of the ten most important things that will probably wind up in your story." She did. "OK, spend a little time with the list and put one star next to the most important stuff." When she showed me her list, sure enough, she had placed one star next to each of the ten items.

Even the dimmest bulb in the teaching chandelier could see that this writer had problems with selection. This is often the case for researchers who have great skill at hunting and gathering but almost no ability to sort through their piles to find special value. I learned about this problem from one of the greatest editors I've ever known, the late Steve Lovelady, who worked with two of America's most influential investigative reporters, Donald Barlett and James Steele. "I had this recurring nightmare," Lovelady said, "that the two of them would walk into my office like robots with stacks and stacks of files in their hands, saying, 'There are many evil people in the world.

Here are the names of some of them.'" But which ones should we put in the magazine, guys? That was Steve's special gift to writers, to help them separate what was important and good from what was really important and especially good. Mine your material, perhaps with the help of a friend or colleague, for the handful of gold nuggets that will make your story shine. Mark each of those with three stars.

Copy the best material you have and put the other material aside.

You may need two or three boxes. The first will contain material you know you'll want to use, and you'll want to make a copy of that material as backup. Another box holds the stuff you probably won't use. The third will hold things you are not yet sure about.

Anyone who has ever read a big pile of applications to a program or entries to a contest will recognize this strategy. It takes time to cut something down to size. As a contest judge, I would use three symbols to indicate the equivalent of yes, no, maybe. It is never hard to select the best 10 percent of the entries, or the 10 percent at the bottom of the barrel. What's hard, of course, is what's left in the middle. There, it becomes painful to cut. In high school, I received a uniform to play on the varsity baseball team, but when new rules required a cut from twenty-six players to twenty-four, I was the last player to be cut. It still hurts.

Perhaps a better metaphor for this strategy is a form of "triage." When treating those wounded in battle, the medics often divide the injured into three groups: can help, can't help, can help if there is time. A sad and often tragic form of yes, no, maybe. Don't waste time with your worst material. It's always there in the "No" box if you need to get at it. Begin with the "Yes" material and follow where it leads you.

Create a random list of the ten most important things that will be in your story.

When you know your material well enough, brainstorm a list of the most interesting or important elements. Once you have a list, begin to move things around, looking for some kind of order. It will go easier if you don't try to give any items priority at first; better to begin the list as the elements come to you. I'll start such a list right now, on my conversion from six decades as a New York Yankees fan to cheering for our local baseball team, the Tampa Bay Rays.

- The day I knew I would change allegiance.
- Reactions of family members who feel some betrayal.
- How the Rays went from worst to first.
- What happens when the Yankees play the Rays?
- When I go to Yankee Stadium, will I root for the Yankees?
- Is it possible to root against players you once thought you loved?
- When I started to give away my Yankees gear...

And so on. The benefits of this compilation become obvious immediately: I've discovered topics I did not even know I wanted to write about, along with some happy juxtapositions, such as the accumulation of team gear as a test of your fidelity as a fan.

Next comes a period of quiet contemplation to study the

list, expand it, move elements around, begin to imagine a better order — all in the hopes of discovering the best bone structure for the story itself.

Now make a list of the five most important things.

If you have a list of ten, cut it to five. Force yourself to make hard choices — or get a pal to help you. If you ever write for me, I'll ask you to winnow a list of ten to five; from five to three; from three to one. Remember the analogy of the funnel: large opening at the top, small one at the bottom. The entire process is one of distillation, of boiling it down, cooling it off, boiling it down again, until you arrive at the essence of your idea or argument.

If you get your list down to five, it may be time to look for an order. The number five is helpful to writers because it offers the potential for a strong top, three levels in the middle, and a bottom that can support it all. Without much work, you can turn the five elements of your list into potential parts of the story, creating not a complicated outline but a simple plan.

If you've ever struggled with an outline and all its determinative details, try out a five-part plan, something you can write on a single piece of paper or even an index card. Such work can be a bit abstract, which is why some writers find it tough sledding. When I am at the point where I can complete this task, my thinking sharpens, my energy rises, my words become more precise and more suited to the topic. Just from something like this:

A. Begin with the moment of my conversion from Yankees fan to Rays fan.
B. Flash back to childhood when I first fell in love with the Yankees.

C. Recall a past moment of family Yankees celebration (maybe 1996 World Series).
D. Describe the excitement of the season when the Rays went from worst to first.
E. Re-create the explosive joy in St. Pete when the Rays beat the Red Sox for the American League pennant.

I've used the same strategy for writing fiction, in this case a newspaper serial titled *Ain't Done Yet:*

A. Beaten-down journalist Max Timlin agrees to accept a freelance assignment to investigate a millennial cult.
B. Max learns the real nature of his new editor's secret interest in the cult.
C. Max meets the cult leader, with surprising and disastrous results.
D. With the help of a beautiful young computer researcher, Max discovers the true identity of the cult leader and sets out to thwart his terrorist plans.
E. On the night of the new millennium, in a ferocious storm, Max engages the cult leader in a final battle to the death—atop the Sunshine Skyway Bridge.

Create files for each of the most important elements.

Once you have decided on the most important parts, you can create a file for each and divide your best material into these compartments. Many writers for many reasons develop electronic files to store their most important stuff, using advanced technical skills to move and manage and massage material therein. They know the value of "backing up" their files by erecting a safety net against a computer catastrophe.

That said, I retain my affection for paper copies of my notes and clippings, stored in manila folders or hanging files, because I can better see everything at once, gaining both visual and tactile mastery over material that could easily fly out of control.

I learned this strategy from John McPhee, one of America's most honored nonfiction authors. In his introduction to *The John McPhee Reader,* editor William Howarth described McPhee's working methods in detail. In an era before word processing, McPhee would type out his notes, photocopy them, look for key subject areas, separate his notes into those areas, and store material in file folders that came to represent book chapters and other divisions of the text. Writers need to *manipulate* their material, a word that comes from the Latin for "by hand."

Write down the ten most important parts on index cards.

Ten seconds ago, I learned something quite interesting about the word *index:* It derives from the Latin word for forefinger, as in your index finger, or, as we called it in kindergarten, Mister Pointer. So an index card, figuratively, points you to a place you want to go, something you want to find. (Not until this moment have I ever associated the *index* in *index finger* with the one in *index card.*)

Getting your arms around a big project requires you to create an index or a table of contents for your story, naming each important part. I still keep the index cards I used in 1996 to create a twenty-nine-part serial narrative titled "Three Little Words." That stack contained about 125 cards. And because it was a story rather than a report, the basic structural elements were scenes. I read through hundreds of pages of notes from hours and hours of transcribed interviews, and each time I came across a scene, I would create a card for it. On that card I'd record a brief description of the scene: "Jane learns in hospital room that Mick has AIDS." I included directions pointing to the appropriate spot in my files: "I—27" meant I could find the notes to this scene in file I on page 27.

The number of cards grows or shrinks as you make important decisions along the way. Each decision is tentative. I don't think there is a noun form of the adjective *tentative,* but there should be one: tentativity. Your index cards are not promissory notes. You retain the freedom of—yes, there is a real noun form—tentativeness.

Play with the cards to find a meaningful order.

Lay out your cards on a rug or a bulletin board. Look for a coherent order, where the parts fit nicely. You can always change your mind later. If you are writing a story, for example, you will be using time elements to help shape the narrative. Even if scenes appear in chronological order, the writer still must decide where to begin and where to end each scene. Will a scene be this long: ——————? Or this long:——? Or as long as the two combined? Plan for those moments when time will not run in a straight line but will cycle back. So the story can begin with the scene of a funeral on a rocky beach, which can flash back to the disclosure of the secret illness in a Spanish hospital, which can flash back again to when the couple first met in a high school classroom in Michigan.

I tend not to write books from beginning to end. I build

momentum by writing on a subtopic that interests me, say the use of an ellipsis (...) to create suspense in a short story. The next day I might write about the difference between *a* and *the*. Then, perhaps, I'll draft an essay on Orwell's use of language in *1984*. The reason for this, if I may borrow a cliché, is to strike while the iron is hot, or to write what I want to write when I'm ready to write it. For me, this eliminates interludes of indecision that often slow me down.

I may wind up with thirty or forty essays on writing or grammar strategies all thrown into one big box, not separated by content or theme. Enter the index cards. I will create an annotated card for each of the essays, then say to myself: "OK, I've got these thirty writing strategies, each one on a card. What kind of categories should I put them in? For *Writing Tools* it turned out to be "Nuts and Bolts," "Special Effects," "Blueprints," and "Useful Habits." For *The Glamour of Grammar* it turned out to be "Words," "Points," "Standards," "Meaning," and "Purpose." It took a long time to arrive at those seemingly simple categories. I got by with a little help from my index card friends.

Pull out file #1 and card #1 and start writing.

You've got to start somewhere. Perhaps part one will become part three before you are through. But try taking cards in order to see where it leads you. You may want to try a preliminary step, that is, to write the introduction to your project without reference to any books, files, or cards. This will be a wonderful test for you and your methods. If you have gone to the trouble of gathering and now organizing your materials, you will be learning your topic every step of the way. There's a bit of Zen philosophy there: Organize your notes so you don't have to refer to them.

I might do the same for each chapter. Let's say file #1 and card #1 read: "I can't think of anything to write." I then may open the file and graze through it, just to remind myself of the valuable resources I've compiled. Then I can swing my chair to the left and write as fast as I can what I think I know about finding story ideas. That makes the next part easy. I can now go through my file bit by bit. From it I can fact-check what I've written, or add an anecdote I'd forgotten, or harvest a quotation that helps me make my point.

Write a mission statement for your story, listing the three things readers will take from your work.

Write yourself a note about your hopes for your writing project. What are you trying to accomplish? Before you know exactly what you want to put into a story, imagine what you want your reader to get out of it. Such commentary can appear in a book as a foreword or afterword, often written last. Writing it first helps you test your thesis. If it proves strong enough, it can guide how you organize and execute the rest of the work.

Here, for example, is the preface to the book *Crazy* by Pete Earley:

> I had no idea.
>
> I've been a journalist for more than thirty years, a reporter for the *Washington Post*, the author of several non-fiction books about crime and punishment and society, some of them award-winning, even best-selling. I've interviewed murderers and spies, judges and prosecutors, always

seeking the truth and attempting to convey it so that readers can see the people and the events for themselves — can understand not only what happened, also why.

But I was always on the outside looking in. I had no idea what it was like to be on the inside looking out. Until my son Mike was declared mentally ill.

What follows is both a personal story and a remarkable act of reportage, a view into the horrible ways we treat the mentally ill in American society, along with some directions for reform. "I hope the book provides some extra light and clarity," writes Earley. "I hope it will inspire you to action, for the stories told here, in this day and age, are extraordinary and worthy of your attention. If it could happen to my family, it could happen to yours."

—.—

Finding Focus

Finding a focus is writing's central act. A strong focus requires a keen knowledge of what the work is about, an insight often reflected in titles, theme statements, captions, summaries, conclusions, "nut" paragraphs, and the like. The writer looks for this defining idea or language from the beginning of the process but often finds it late, too late to do it justice.

Looking for a focus is not searching for a needle in a haystack. If it feels that way, your topic may be too broad. It will be easier to find that needle in, say, a hatbox. To abuse that needle metaphor again, I want my focus to be sharp and pointed, something I can write on an index card:

- Athletic women are especially prone to knee injuries.
- Some former opponents of the military draft now support it.
- Millions of homeowners owe more on their mortgages than their houses are worth.

The above statements are in focus, but taken at a wide angle. They can also be expressed as close-ups:

- Gina Dworkin's left knee is a battle-scarred standard for her devotion to soccer.
- Jonathan Malone once thought about burning his draft card. Now it hangs over his desk, a constant reminder of a mission he has embraced: restoration of the military draft.
- The Blynken family can barely afford flood insurance for their house, which will not rescue them from being "underwater" and in foreclosure.

In modern parlance, the word *focus* seems borrowed from the visual arts, especially photography or cinematography, where the artist tries to keep images in focus, except when working a special effect. I prefer the root meaning, where *focus* was the Latin word for "hearth," the heart of the household. The tribe gathers around the campfire or fireplace to find warmth, to gain the sustenance of food, to converse, to hear a yarn or two. It is a shared experience, and the writer hopes that a sharp focus will help readers find a shared experience of language, message, and meaning.

Problems covered in this chapter:

CENTER WON'T HOLD

It may surprise readers of finished stories to know that the writer does not always know what the story is *really* about. Ask writers that question and see how fuzzy the answers can be. What you get is not a sharp statement of theme, but a reiteration of topic: "My story is really about the oil spill in the Gulf of Mexico," to which a friend could respond, "So what about it?" The failure to understand what the story is about can only result in indecision for the writer and confusion for the reader. A hazy focus will prevent the writer from making good selections from the material gathered. It will stand in the way of a clean blueprint of a story's architecture and details. A sharp focus should be a result of all the good work you've done so far. It will make your remaining tasks easier and more to the point.

NOT KNOWING HOW TO BEGIN

Many writers refer to the beginning of a story as the "lead." Even young children understand the concept, that the top of a work should lead the reader into the body of the story. To do that, the writer must capture the reader's attention right away, with content or language both interesting and important.

That is not an easy task, which is why writers can lose their nerve. "It's the beginnings that are hard," critic and author Susan Sontag told the *Paris Review*. "I always begin with a great sense of dread and trepidation. Nietzsche says that the decision to start writing is like leaping into a cold lake."

The length, purpose, and style of a lead depend on the genre. The first line in a student's college entrance essay has to grab the busy admissions officer by the throat. The first lines of a contemporary novel should compel the reader in a bookstore to buy the book. Colum McCann closed his deal with me with the opening passage of *Let the Great World Spin:*

> Those who saw him hushed. On Church Street. Liberty. Cortlandt. West Street. Fulton. Vesey. It was a silence that heard itself, awful and beautiful. Some thought at first that it must have been a trick of the light, something to do with the weather, an accident of shadowfall. Others figured it might be the perfect city joke—stand around and point upward, until people gathered, tilted their heads, nodded, affirmed, until all were staring upward at nothing at all, like waiting for the end of a Lenny Bruce gag. But the longer they watched, the surer they were. He stood at the very edge of the building, shaped dark against the gray of the morning. A window washer maybe. Or a construction worker. Or a jumper.

Most books open much more slowly, often for good literary reasons. Still, I've never met a writer who sought instant rejection by a bored, distracted, or time-starved reader.

CAN'T DECIDE WHAT TO PICK

Inexperienced writers empty their notebooks into their stories. The pros, on the other hand, use a small percentage of their research, a process of selection in support of the focus. If a writer is unable to select between the "good" and the "pretty good," it may be because the focus is still...out of focus. The writer may have to retreat a step or two, gathering new material to gain a clearer understanding of what the story is about.

Choosing one detail often requires cutting another. An intellectual and emotional bond develops between author and material, but there comes a time when the writer must learn to let go. For the disciplined writer this separation can come early in the process, when the writer is making choices about reporting and research strategies. The story will not work, say, with a cast of fifteen characters, so which five are worthy of the writer's and reader's attention? Another chance to select the best material and leave the rest behind comes halfway through the process. A final chance arrives late in the game, when a ruthless determination is required to cut any element that does not reinforce the point, theme, or focus of the writing.

REFLECT

- At what stage of the process do you begin to discover the focus of your story?
- Do you have to write your lead sentence or introduction — and get it just right — before you can write anything else? Or can you dive into the middle?
- Would it be hard or easy for you to answer the question "What is your story *really* about?"
- How much of your working materials appears in a report or story?
- Ask that same question of other writers you know and record what you discover.
- Have you ever found it impossible to cut something from a story, even when it didn't necessarily support your focus?

7

—•—

I don't know what my story is really about.

Limit the scope of the topic.

Thinking about the scope of the story—the width of your topic—will help you figure out your focus. From early in the process, from the time of the assignment or the hatching of the idea, and before you finish your research, look for the sharpest possible angle of approach. If you wait until the drafting stage, you may miss the chance to gather the evidence you need to make your point. In other words, *don't write about education but about a school, or a classroom, or a student.*

The writer can take a big topic, such as boys falling behind girls in school, and mark off a territory within that topic and build a fence around it. You will not write a book about the struggles of boys in the twenty-first century, at least not yet, but you could write something focused on the effects on boys of compulsive video game playing. When you get there, you can pull the fence in tighter to focus on the negative effects. Even there, the fence could contract to include only the negative effects of violent video games. Before you are finished, you may reduce your efforts and interests to a particular game (Grand Theft Auto) and a particular group of boys (nonreaders).

This is old and reliable advice: Limit the topic. The wider the topic, the more research material you'd have to draw from. But you'll soon discover so much research available that you can't get a handle on it, or you can't figure out where to start. You'll gather more interesting and relevant stuff when you whittle the topic down to a shape you begin to recognize.

Ask yourself over and over, "What is this story really about?"

That question has become a mantra among the writers and writing teachers who work at Poynter. Chip Scanlan, borrowing from teacher and editor Lucille DeView, introduced a speed-writing exercise into seminars that asked students to write for ten minutes about their "favorite dessert." I rolled my eyes the first time I heard of this idea, but it turned out to produce interesting personal stories, narratives that wind their way into themes of history, culture, ethnicity, family, love, and legacies.

Most professional writers can generate about two hundred words of copy in that time, just enough to offer answers to the magic question. "What is your story about?" we ask the writers in the room. The class clowns respond, "Tapioca pudding" or "Hostess CupCakes" or "My grandma's pineapple upside-down cake."

"OK, smart aleck, what is your story *really* about?"

It's often way too early to answer, but the writer still benefits from thinking it through. Perhaps when the writer thought of a favorite dessert, it reminded her of the first person she shared it with, or the person who prepared it, or the place where it was first discovered. Lest you think this is some sort of wimpy literary exercise, remember that Marcel Proust wrote more than a thousand pages in volume one of *Remembrance of Things Past,* a novel that flowed from the simple act of biting into a favorite cookie — the madeleine.

The first efforts to discover your deeper meaning will be expressed in thematic abstractions: "It's really about fear...," or comfort, or home, or family, or courage, or loyalty, or denial, or the hundred other themes writers depend upon most often. Remember, a topic — exotic pets — is not a story. A story is when a woman's pet chimpanzee attacks and disfigures her best friend and neighbor — and then tries to kill the owner.

Try writing a lead sentence that captures the focus.

John McPhee calls the lead the flashlight that shines down into the story. Write a sentence or a paragraph or even a passage designed to help readers see what's up ahead or round the bend: "The sport of shuffleboard, with a rich history in St. Petersburg, is undergoing a revival thanks to a group not usually associated with this haven for retirees: young people."

It's not possible from this single sentence to predict everything that may come in the story, but readers learn enough from this lead to make reasonable guesses: that the story will have a section on the history of shuffleboard, on the track over time of its popularity, and on the surprising interest from the young, who must be observed and interviewed about their new favorite sport.

"Maybe to an alligator, Jeff Quincy tastes like chicken." That might be a fun lead to a story about a gator trainer who made a wrong move and had one of his reptiles bite down on his arm. But there are many other choices or directions: "What's it feel like to have a thousand pounds of toothy pressure bite down on your arm? Ask gator trainer Jeff Quincy." Editors or readers may prefer one approach to another, but the act of writing a lead is by definition a focusing move.

I know writers who write several experimental leads before they settle on one that best captures the focus. Such experimentation is not extravagant. Each tentative lead teaches the writer something about the unrealized potential in the draft. Writing a good beginning can become a kind of contract with the reader: If you find this paragraph both interesting and important, I promise the rest of the story will be just like that.

Write a six-word theme statement.

There is something of a six-word movement afoot. Write a story in six words. Or a vision statement. Or a mission statement. Shakespeare seems to have stumbled onto the strategy of the six-word summary: "The Queen, my lord, is dead" or "To be or not to be" or "Out, vile jelly! Where is thy luster now?" Okay, that's eight words.

Here are examples of six-word theme statements from a variety of stories:

- "Real cowboys don't ride fake bulls."
- "Culture, not race, produces great athletes."

- "More women than men reach ninety."
- "The fleas come with the dog."
- "Baby, we were born to run."
- "Check yourself before you wreck yourself."
- "Parents won't let dying children go."
- "U.S. forces kill Osama Bin Laden."

The moral that ends a fable has that six-word feel to it: "Necessity is the mother of invention." In fiction, a brief summary or description can evolve into a title that can be expressed in fewer than six words: *The Postman Always Rings Twice,* by James M. Cain; "A Perfect Day for Bananafish," by J. D. Salinger; *True Grit,* by Charles Portis.

A theme statement, of whatever length, need not appear in a story to do its work. Because a theme is often expressed in abstract language, it can lend a story altitude but not particularity. In other words, the theme "tells," when the writer may be looking for opportunities to "show." Variation helps, especially in longer works that carry multiple themes.

A version of the theme statement can go almost anywhere in the story: at the very top, down four or five paragraphs to illuminate the lead, right in the middle, or at the end. Such a versatile tool can be a godsend to the writer.

Make sure all the evidence in your story points to a single idea or conclusion.

I remember the day I read a reprint of an investigative series in the *Providence Journal.* The first sentence read, "Jewelry work in Rhode Island is life at the bottom of industrial America." That is not written in a neutral or disinterested voice. But neither is it an editorial opinion. I would call it, simply, an informed conclusion. As I read the story, I came to see all the evidence (poor working conditions, exploitation of children) that made that conclusion inevitable.

If I have come to believe that many vulnerable patients never get colonoscopies because of their inhibitions about their bodies, I have a responsibility to prove it. I interview a woman who refuses to take the test, even though her doctor keeps advising her to do so. "That's an exit down there, not an entrance," she says. Her attitude is one tiny piece of evidence. I need much more to make the story persuasive. I must marshal my evidence in a disciplined way, using any quote, anecdote, or statistic that supports the point. Any extraneous bit deserves to be snipped like a malignant polyp.

Cut the elements least supportive of your focus.

Not all evidence is equal. If you can identify the weakest evidence, what is left—your strongest stuff—can support a sharp focus. But what makes evidence weak?

- It will appear in the story only because of your interest in it.
- You will find yourself making lame excuses for its inclusion.
- It is neither important nor interesting.
- You will keep moving it farther and farther down in the story.
- It is impossible to write it clearly and quickly for a general audience.

- A test reader will begin to lose interest when she gets to that part.
- *You* begin to lose interest when you get to that part.
- It will not click with other elements of evidence to form a coherent whole.

When you dump such sludge, you are left with material that is lean, clean, compelling, crucial, and persuasive.

List three things that your story is about. Which is most important?

What is the "theme" of *Hamlet*? Or of *Moby Dick*? Or of *The Catcher in the Rye*? When I was eighteen years old, I could have given pretty good answers to those questions. When I was twenty-six years old, newly minted PhD in hand, I'm sure I could have given very good, even elegant answers. Now, at the age of sixty-three, I'm not so sure. I've come to think that literary themes are overrated. In a work of any length, a critic can find evidence to spin out a half-dozen themes.

Shakespeare scholar Richard Levin taught me to debunk heavy-handed thematic analysis, reducing most so-called transcendent themes into straightforward statements. What's the theme of the song "Eleanor Rigby"? The Beatles deliver it in the chorus. To paraphrase the Four Mop Tops: The world is filled with lonely people looking for someone to love, and to love them.

It turns out that literary works include lots of statements, a fact that makes me more comfortable with themes plural than with some singular defining idea. *The Catcher in the Rye* is about the loss of innocence through adolescence; or it's about the phoniness of sophisticated adult society; or it's about New York City as a microcosm of urban neurosis; or it's about all of those things—and more.

If you can't say yet what your story is about, create a list of things it *could* be about. Which items on your list are the most persuasive? Such strategic thinking can lead you to a workable focus.

Ask yourself, "What feeling do I want to leave with the reader?"

You cannot control how your reader feels, but you can influence this through your choices. Imagine the most desirable effect on the reader. Write your story with that result in mind. At a recent lunch, a group of writers sat down to discuss our strong feelings about the award-winning novel *Let the Great World Spin*, by Irish author Colum McCann. As always, each of us brought to the reading some version of our autobiography. It seemed to matter whether (1) you were from New York (I am); (2) you were afraid of heights (I am); (3) you had grown up Catholic (check); (4) you had ever been near the Twin Towers before or after 9/11 (double check).

More compelling, though, were the shared impressions of the novel from a diverse group of readers. We all felt that the novel, set in New York in 1974 and beginning with the real story of the French daredevil who walked across a cable stretched between the two towers, was really a story about the spirit of New York City in the aftermath of the destruction of those towers on 9/11/2001.

We also thought the book felt like a generous love letter to New York City, even though it was set in a time before the city was "cleaned up." In spite of the myriad problems represented by the city, the author shows characters benefiting from the rich web of personal and social connections people need to survive in any metropolis. There is no Superman or Batman to save us from our darker angels, McCann seemed to be saying. There is only us reaching out to help, or to seek help. The author never once tells us this. His gives us something better, lifelike characters with whom we can share feelings of empathy and sympathy.

If you had been able to overhear that conversation about the novel in the Bella Brava restaurant, you would have listened to the evidence each of us brought to the support of those feelings and ideas. It was as if the author created a map for us, a trail of meaning and sensibility that would connect readers the way he connected the characters in his novel. In our novel.

List questions your story will answer for the reader.

List those questions in random order. Now choose which questions are most important and see if your story is focused enough to answer them. Here is a hypothetical list of questions for a story about the popular television show *Glee:*

- Are the singing voices we hear on the television coming from the actors themselves?
- What do people mean when they say *Glee* is the "gayest" show in the history of network television?
- How does a show manage to successfully mix comedy, drama, music, and dance?

- How do actors in their twenties manage to give credible performances as high school students?
- Has the show sparked a growth in the popularity of high school glee clubs and other performance groups?

Those are useful questions, any one of them capable of generating a focused work, but not all of them together. The writer must sort through such a list and test out the various possible angles to find the most productive.

Brainstorm titles for the work.

News editors have this great trick they pull when they can't write a headline or title for a particular story: They bounce the problem back to the writer.

"It's my job to write the story," protests the writer, "and your job to write the headline."

"I'm asking you out of respect. I'm asking you to try to write a title that captures what you think is the focus of the story."

In most cases, the writer can't write a good headline either. Or the writer writes a good headline, but it reflects only a slice of the story. In other words, an unfocused story makes the writing of a title almost impossible. Brainstorming titles can help all the players discover what the story is really about, which often leads to useful deletions and revisions.

Writers should always be thinking of titles. It should not matter whether the writer is asked or not, or whether the writer has any say in or influence on decisions about titles. Simply put, if the writer can't come up with a decent title, the task of finding a focus has not yet been completed.

Think of the power of song titles. "Respect," "(I Can't Get No) Satisfaction," "I Heard It Through the Grapevine," "The Star-Spangled Banner," "Begin the Beguine," "You Are My Sunshine," "Hound Dog," "Tutti Frutti"—just reciting the titles evokes most of what you need to know about the songs: tone, rhythm, lyrics, rhyme, theme, attitude, and much more.

So if the lead of a story can be described as a flashlight, then think of a great title as a lighthouse that guides the reader past shoals of confusion and indirection toward a safe harbor of understanding and meaning.

8

—•—

I struggle with the beginning.

Collect examples of good beginnings. Read them for inspiration.

If you want to write short form, read good short stories. If you want to write better endings, read better endings. And if you want to write better leads or openings or beginnings or intros (different writers use different terms), start reading and collecting the best you can find.

To take this strategy a step higher, pay attention to any form of expression that depends upon a good beginning. What constitutes a good start in a poem, a movie, a weather report, a song?

The benefits to the writer are many. Just as a chef learns what good food tastes like, so a writer must taste a lot of work to find a full range of possible strategic options. Your first reaction may be "There are so many different approaches that seem to work, it's impossible for me to tell which one is 'better' or how it constitutes a strategy." Consider that a strength of the process. Ultimately you will have a toolbox for lead writing. It will contain some of the tools in this chapter, no doubt, and many others you will discover along the way.

Check these out:

- "So. The Spear-Danes in days gone by / and the kings who ruled them had courage and greatness." *Beowulf,* translated by Seamus Heaney. (Begin in the historical past.)
- "The unusual events described in this chronicle occurred in 194– at Oran." *The Plague,* by Albert Camus. (Omitting that final digit suggests mystery, what can't be known or told.)
- "All this happened, more or less. The war parts, anyway, are pretty much true. One guy I knew really *was* shot in Dresden for taking a teapot that wasn't his." *Slaughterhouse-Five,* by Kurt Vonnegut. ("All this" usually describes what has come before; this version points to what is up ahead.)
- "Alexey Fyodorovitch Karamazov was the third son of Fyodor Pavlovitch Karamazov, a landowner well known in our district in his own day, and still remembered among us owing to his gloomy and tragic death, which happened thirteen years ago, and which I shall describe in its proper place." *The Brothers Karamazov,* by Fyodor Dostoevsky, translated by Constance Garnett. ("Gloomy and tragic death" plants the seeds for further revelations.)

In each of these, the author has chosen a particular effect to launch the work. To write good beginnings, you have to read many. You will discover they come in great varieties: long and short; elaborate and plain; conclusive and exploratory. "First sentences are marked by compression," write Stanley Fish in *How to Write a Sentence.* "They do a lot of work in a short time."

Ask yourself: What is most important here?

When we talk about that critical facility called "the writer's judgment," we usually mean the ability to separate in nonfiction what is important from what is merely interesting. To discover and report, in other words, what matters. Bad writing spends too much time persuading us that something of great interest (say, the infidelities of a movie star) is somehow important. The more responsible scribe prefers to take important matters and render them in ways that will interest readers.

Melvin Mencher, a legendary teacher at the Columbia Graduate School of Journalism, asked his students to judge the relative importance and interest of events against a set of values such as timeliness, proximity, conflict, prominence, currency, impact, and even the bizarre. The best stories, especially ones written in the public interest, derive from more than one of these standards. These questions will also help:

- What matters to you (the writer)?
- What do you think matters most to readers?
- What part of the story is likely to have the greatest impact?
- What might change the way the reader sees or experiences the world?

Let's apply these to a recent anniversary, thirty years since the destruction of the Sunshine Skyway Bridge spanning Tampa Bay. A sudden morning storm blew a huge freighter into the bridge, destroying most of it and sending thirty-five people to their deaths. Another bridge was built to replace it.

What matters to me? That most of the deaths associated with the bridge have come not from that accident in 1980, but from suicides committed by people jumping two hundred feet off the new span. We put concrete bumpers in the bay to protect the bridge against big ships. What can we do to help those who seek out this precipice to end their lives?

Such reflection might lead to a straightforward numbers lead: "When the freighter *Summit Venture* plowed into the Sunshine Skyway Bridge thirty years ago today, thirty-five motorists and passengers plunged to their deaths. The new bridge remains a death trap, not as a target for freighters, but as a temptation for the depressed and desperate. More than eighty deaths have resulted from suicide leaps from the top of the Skyway."

Ask yourself, "What is most interesting?"

Interesting things are not always important, but they can help move the reader toward a topic of great relevance. Look for the fact, detail, or anecdote that one person is likely to pass along to another. While there is no foolproof formula for interestingness, there are some reliable topics: funny pets and other animals; clever or obnoxious little children; sex in all its varieties, implications, and consequences; celebrities at their worst; plastic surgeries gone wrong; miracle cures. If you need more, just buy a supermarket tabloid and check their stories against my list.

But let's not get snooty here. Consider this lead from a page-one story in the *Wall Street Journal* by Michael M. Phillips. The headline: "Phone Hex."

> It was a first date, and Lee Cruz was necking in the car. In midtussle, she jostled the cell phone in her purse and, without realizing it, she triggered speed-dial No. 2, which rang up her ex-boyfriend.
>
> He answered and listened in. For 22 minutes.
>
> One thing she says struck her eavesdropping ex as especially memorable: "No, no," she told her new beau. "You're a married man."

It's important to note that this is not a story about infidelity, but about one of the quirks of the information age: the ways in which cell phones get us into trouble.

Music and copyrights have been much in the news, but rather than begin with an explanation of a legal battle, the *Journal's* Lisa Bannon offered a scene from Diablo Day Camp, where a troop of Girl Scouts dance the Macarena — without music:

> They spin, wiggle and shake. They bounce for two minutes.
>
> In silence.
>
> "Yesterday I told them we could be sued if we played the music," explains Teesie King, camp co-director and a volunteer mom. "So they decided they'd learn it without the music."

Conflict, while overused in many media contexts, generates interest and draws an audience. "Nothing moves forward in a story except through conflict," writes Robert McKee in his book *Story*. "Conflict is to storytelling what sound is to music."

Decide what the reader needs to know first.

Scholar Louise Rosenblatt once asked her readers to imagine that instead of taking our daily medicine, we ingested poison by mistake. Down the hatch. Gulp. You see the poison warning on the bottle. What would you do? The label on the back of that bottle may be the most important thing you ever read or, if written badly, the last thing you will ever read.

No time for flowery language or subordinate clauses. The responsible writer must offer emergency advice: Call poison control at this number; induce vomiting (or not); drink milk (or not); call 911. This suggests that we should add "urgency" to our list of values that influence literary or editorial judgment. While all deadlines are not equally death-inducing, some require vigilance and action:

"If you owe the government taxes and fail to file by midnight tonight, you may be in trouble. After all, the feds never got Al Capone for being a mob chief and killer. They got him for tax evasion."

Or "With a possible Category Three hurricane headed our way, it's time to take action to protect yourselves, your property, and your pets."

Or, much less serious but still relevant, "Only a handful of tickets remain on sale for American Stage's wildly popular production of *Hair*. If you want in, act now."

There will be times when what readers need to know first is not urgent but a necessary foundation upon which to build an argument. They may need to know, for example, what doctors consider a hospital emergency before the writer can then make a case that the resources of the local hospital are being overtaxed.

In fiction, the urgency to read on does not come from information, but from effects such as:

- An engaging voice. Saul Bellow in *Herzog:* "If I am out of my mind, it's all right with me, thought Moses Herzog."
- A curious mood. John Steinbeck in *Cannery Row:* "Cannery Row in Monterey in California is a poem, a stink, a grating noise, a quality of light, a tone, a habit, a nostalgia, a dream."
- An invitation into an intriguing new world. Amy Tan in *The Joy Luck Club:* "The old woman remembered a swan she had bought many years ago in Shanghai for a foolish sum. This bird, boasted the market vendor, was once a duck that stretched its neck in hopes of becoming a goose, and now look! — it is too beautiful to eat."

Find a clue to plant early to foreshadow meaningful themes and events.

I want to offer a distinction that helps me better understand what should go at the top of one of my stories. Consider the difference between *foreshadowing* and *foreboding*. Let's start with dictionary definitions:

foreboding: "1. a sense of impending evil or misfortune. 2. an evil omen; a portent."
foreshadowing: "an indication or suggestion beforehand."

Clearly, there is a difference here, at least in connotation. *To forebode* seems the darker verb. Let's take two movies as examples. *The Blair Witch Project* is filled with foreboding, whether expressed through unknown sounds in the darkness or spooky symbols left in trees. Contrast those effects to the early scenes in *Raiders of the Lost Ark.* Remember when Indiana Jones steals the sacred statue and then has to escape from all the traps in the cave? He finally gets into a small plane and, thinking he's almost safe, looks down to find a snake at his feet. Remember what he says? "I hate snakes!" A not too subtle foreshadowing of a later scene in which he must descend into a tomb crawling with...you guessed it.

Those who know Chaucer's bawdy *Canterbury Tales* will remember the comic villain Absolom in the gloriously funny "Miller's Tale." We learn early in the fable that the fussy cleric is "somewhat squeamish about farting." This chicken will come home to roost when Absolom is tricked into kissing the rear end of his love interest.

You may want to make a list of the two or three most important revelations in your story, and rewrite your opening to foreshadow one.

Think of a scene or anecdote that captures what your story is about.

An anecdote is a "short account of an interesting or humorous incident," derived from a Greek word that means "unpublished." I think the sense is "*previously* unpublished," and anecdotes about friends or celebrities often trail a whiff of gossip behind them, items that surprise or delight because heard for the first time. (At least six times a year, I hear someone pronounce the word "antidote.")

Here's an anecdote from Gene Weingarten of the *Washington Post* on *Doonesbury* creator Garry Trudeau: "He is a millionaire many times over, but Jane [his wife, former TV anchor Jane Pauley] cuts his hair." His wife cuts his hair. A five-word anecdote. We also learn that Trudeau and his pals like to go to really bad movies: "The best worst recent choice was a Lou Diamond Phillips flick where a car exploded and then, in a later scene, the same car drove off a cliff."

The difference between a scene and an anecdote is crucial for the writer and the reader. If a story begins with a scene — especially in a work of fiction — there's a great chance that another scene will follow, drawing upon the previous one for its relevance. So *Charlotte's Web* by E. B. White begins in the kitchen of a farmhouse:

"Where's Papa going with that ax?" said Fern to her mother as they were setting the table for breakfast.

"Out to the hoghouse," replied Mrs. Arable. "Some pigs were born last night."

"I don't see why he needs an ax," continued Fern, who was only eight.

"Well," said her mother, "one of the pigs is a runt. It's very small and weak, and it will never amount to anything. So your father has decided to do away with it."

"Do *away* with it?" shrieked Fern. "You mean *kill* it? Just because it's smaller than the others?"

Thus begins one of the most touching and popular books for children, enjoyed by generations of parents as well. That scene kicks off a narrative about the cycle of nature and related issues of life and death.

Anecdotes tend to be more self-contained. The writer may begin a story with an anecdote about a man who smoked cigarettes in bed and died in a fire, but we may never see him again, because the story is not about the man, but about fires, or sleeping, or cigarettes.

Choose a main character and decide when your readers will meet that person.

In most cases, your main character will come first in your narrative. There are creative exceptions, to be sure. But it makes great sense for the writer to point a camera at the character whose actions will be governed by the focus of the story. We just encountered this strategy in the passage from *Charlotte's Web*, in which we get word of a little pig about to get the ax.

Narrative time and circumstances may determine that the entrance of the hero will be a bit delayed. Shakespeare is quite good at this, understanding how the appearance onstage of a famous actor can electrify the audience. Thus, *Hamlet* begins with the prince offstage and the ghost of his father appearing to the castle's guards. *Romeo and Juliet* begins with a street fight between the Montagues and the Capulets, setting the stage for an entrance by star-crossed lover Romeo.

But the default position is that the protagonist appears early, sometimes right out of the chute, as does one of the cowboys in Annie Proulx's *Brokeback Mountain*:

> Ennis Del Mar wakes up before five, wind rocking the trailer, hissing in around the aluminum door and window

frames. The shirts hanging on a nail shudder slightly in the draft. He gets up, scratching the grey wedge of belly and pubic hair, shuffles to the gas burner, pours leftover coffee in a chipped enamel pan; the flame swathes it in blue.

If the circumstances are interesting enough, the author can begin a story by turning the camera on himself, a strategy used by Jean-Dominique Bauby in *The Diving Bell and the Butterfly:*

> Through the frayed curtain at my window, a wan glow announces the break of day. My heels hurt, my head weighs a ton, and something like a giant invisible diving bell holds my whole body prisoner.

In both of these cases, the story starts with a single character at the beginning of the day. Both, it turns out, are burdened by a problem the story seeks to solve. The cowboy is a gay man living a secret life in a world of Western machismo. The man in the metaphorical diving bell is trapped in a body devastated by a massive stroke. But we don't know these conflicts yet, so the author must be interesting, even provocative in the use of language to capture and hold the reader.

Ask yourself, "If I were making a movie of my story, what image would the viewer see first?"

You would think that writers growing up in the age of motion pictures and television would develop a propensity for describing things cinematically. This is not the case. Crafting the revealing image is a skill, especially difficult if the writer's goal is to grab the attention of the multitasking reader.

Let's begin with what writing for the cinema actually looks like. Consider this opening sequence taken from the screenplay of *The Seventh Seal* by Ingmar Bergman:

> The night had brought little relief from the heat, and at dawn a hot gust of wind blows across the colorless sea. The knight, Antonius Block, lies prostrate on some spruce branches spread over the fine sand. His eyes are wide-open and bloodshot from lack of sleep.

Consider the variety of camera angles needed to fulfill the promise of those three short sentences. The first one requires an establishing shot, focused on the land- and seascapes. In the second, the camera must move from sky and sea to a single man. A third shot, a close-up, would be necessary to see the blood in the knight's eyes.

Let's examine another warrior, a foil of James Bond, in a similar physical position described to open a popular book, which became a famous movie:

> The naked man who lay splayed out on his face beside the swimming pool might have been dead.

He is not dead until the end of the book, when British secret agent 007 will kill the Soviet assassin Red Grant in *From Russia with Love*.

Here opens a story that began as a newspaper series but grew into a television documentary, a book, and an award-winning film, *Black Hawk Down* by Mark Bowden:

At liftoff, Matt Eversmann said a Hail Mary. He was curled into a seat between two helicopter crew chiefs, the knees of his long legs up to his shoulders. Before him, jammed on both sides of the Black Hawk helicopter, was his "chalk," twelve young men in flak vests over tan desert fatigues.

One way to get your book turned into a movie is to write cinematically.

Find a beginning that appeals to the senses, a detail readers can see, hear, or smell.

We talk about the five senses: sight, sound, smell, taste, and touch. But we also talk about sensitive people who seem to have a "sixth sense." And we use the word *sense* to preface other powers of perception and action: a sense of humor or a sense of decency. Sometimes we use language that cuts across senses, a poetic technique with the name *synesthesia*. When we call a piano solo crisp or a color loud, we are practicing that rhetorical strategy.

Consider Rick Bragg's opening to *I Am a Soldier, Too*, his book about Jessica Lynch, an American soldier captured and rescued in Iraq:

> On most nights of the year, this stretch of country road is only a flat place in the dark. But for a few nights in late summer 2003, it blazed in neon, smelled like smoked sausage, spun sugar and blue-ribbon hogs, and rang with screams of people who had bought a ticket to be scared. They rode the Tilt-A-Whirl, browsed tents of prizewinning fruit preserves and lined up for the cute-baby contest, and if there is such a

thing as a time machine on earth, it must be powered by the Ferris wheel at the Wirt County, West Virginia, Fair. Back from the war, Jessica Lynch asked her mother and father to take her there.

It would be worth the while of any writer to read and reread that passage, study it, read it again aloud, and check off the senses the prose excites. Sight: neon lights, check. Sound: people screaming on the carnival rides, check. Smell: sausage, hogs, cute babies, check. Taste: sausage again, fruit preserves, spun sugar, check. Touch: thrill rides, cotton candy, cuddly babies, check.

Begin the story in the middle of things.

The classical narrative technique in medias res — beginning in the middle of things — has stood the test of centuries. The narrator sidesteps the natural beginning of the story in favor of some middle spot in the narrative:

> Midway in our life's journey, I went astray
> from the straight road and woke to find myself
> alone in a dark wood.

So begins — in the middle of things — Dante's *Inferno,* but he will not be alone in a dark wood for long. He will be guided by his muse in the person of the Roman poet Virgil, author of the epic *The Aeneid,* which also begins, appropriately enough, in the middle of a dangerous journey from the destruction of Troy to the founding of the city of Rome.

Beginning in the middle gives reader and writer two great

advantages: (1) immediate action and a forward thrust into the narrative; (2) the ability to flash back, recovering missing history or context. Anyone who has witnessed the musical *42nd Street* remembers how the dancing starts even before the curtain rises; it then rises only enough to see about thirty pairs of flashing, tapping feet. We don't know it yet, but we are right in the middle of a Broadway audition, a rite of passage for the naive girl who dreams of being a dancing star.

Consider these openings that thrust us into the middle of things:

- "She stood now in the doorway of the plane, suddenly doubting her decision to make her first parachute jump on her seventieth birthday."
- "'What do you mean she's going to be arrested?'"
- "The final vote for the new college president had come down to this. Would the oldest trustee, John Harlin, vote for his best friend, or would he vote for the candidate he thought would be better at the job?"

All readers have trouble "getting into" some stories. Beginning in the middle does away with the throat-clearing narrator and propels us into the action.

9

—•—

I have problems selecting my best stuff.

In the margins of a draft, place brackets next to
any story element that works.

An inhibition to cut relates to an inability to select the best material. Begin then with what works in the story; consider cutting what's left. To do this well requires that the writer transcend the intrinsic negativity built into many writers and editors. From our early schooling through our first professional experiences, we are much better at identifying what needs work in a story than what already works.

Just as we teach students to appreciate the arts, we can help writers appreciate their own best work, and the best work of others. All you need is a bit of guided reverse engineering with a group of friendly writers to discern an author's strategic moves.

When it comes to identifying the best stuff in your own draft, try to see it through the eyes of an ideal reader. Readers know what they like: the detail that reveals all, the character who makes a wrong turn, that delightful reversal saved for the end. These all can earn a bracket in the margins.

Go through your bracketed elements and assign each a value from one to ten.

Even after you've identified some of your best work—and cut other elements—don't be afraid to repeat the process, forcing yourself to distill the best from what you've collected.

The writer-philosopher-king on this topic was none other than Sir Arthur Quiller-Couch, author of a series of lectures on writing delivered to the students of Cambridge University almost a century ago. "Style...is not—can never be—extraneous Ornament....Whenever you feel an impulse to perpetrate a piece of exceptionally fine writing, obey it—whole-heartedly—and delete it before sending your manuscript to press. *Murder your darlings.*"

Those last three words have become both famous and notorious. The word *darlings* refers to loved ones, especially your children. The writer conceives and gives birth to language that he loves. But to share that too ostentatiously with the world is an act of showing off rather than of revealing. Carry that distinction to your own prose. What stands out as acts of revelation? What, on the contrary, calls attention to the literary flourishes of the author?

Continue this process until you have assigned high or low numbers to each bracketed passage.

You can see by now that these methods are more than forms of troubleshooting. They require critical thinking, giving value to some elements of the work over others. By elevating the best, you cause the weaker elements to stand out in sharp relief. Those weaker limbs, which sap the strength of the whole, are ready for pruning.

But what to elevate and what to cut? Good judgment, once again, depends upon the recognition of our two standards: What is important here? What is interesting?

Here is a list of three important things:

- Too many people confuse pornography with human sexuality.
- The damage from oil pollution in the Gulf may take decades to repair.
- A century may pass before another human being sets foot on the moon.

As I type those three, I realize that not only are they important, but they turn out to be interesting as well. That is what every writer in every medium wants most: to be thought of as both interesting and important. In the words of the late editor Cole Campbell, the best work done by writers is about "stuff that matters."

Consider keeping the best of the best — and letting go of the rest.

When Professor Quiller-Couch invited us to murder our darlings, he was not trying to turn us all into verbicidal maniacs. He wanted to teach us the fine art of letting go. Parents, at least some of us, mourn the day when all the little birds have flown, leaving us old crows with an "empty nest." If our words are our children, and we love them all, it doesn't mean that we can't kick them out of the house on occasion, for their good and our own.

The trick is to build your standards as you progress in your writing project. Remember, we invited you to sort through and evaluate the best of your best. Many writers find this method of raising the ante to be easier as they move toward completion and publication. Of course, you will be adding things along the way: a quotation that clarifies, a statistic that leads to a conclusion.

But the simple act of saying, "This is good, that one's good, I like this one" will leave some orphans behind. As long as we're being metaphorically cruel, we can send them off to live the "hard-knock life."

You do not have to "kill" weaker elements in a story. You can "save" them for another story, another day.

So we're not going to put our wayward children into an orphanage or a workhouse after all. It turns out that we can "save" them. Journalists are good at this part of the process. Even if they have to cut their story in half, the other half and all the materials in the notebook can live to see another day.

Journalists may work a beat, after all, so the story about children learning to read is not going to disappear. If it arises again a year from now, the writer will do more research, but she can dip into that older material for sources, anecdotes, quotations, all the elements that she needs to write something new, what is called a "follow" to the original story.

Scholars are notorious for mastering narrower and narrower areas of academic study, writing, and publishing. While doing research on the literature of the Middle Ages, I often bumped into fascinating areas that, while not appropriate for a current project, could be researched and advanced sometime down the road.

Writers can be like locomotives: a little heavy to get going, but when speeding, almost impossible to stop.

If it helps, think of your focus as a knife.

We think of focus as a visual effect, a lens we look through to see the world more clearly. But I have come to see it as a knife, a blade I can use to slice the fat out of a story, leaving behind only the strength of muscle and bone.

A man writes an essay about online plagiarism with a focus on how responsible writers must adopt and adapt standards and practices developed over decades by the traditional media. Along the way, he learns about an author who turned out to be a bigamist, raising two families in different towns. This is juicy stuff, just the kind of anecdote that could spice up a treatise about literary ethics.

But the story is not about bigamy. The writer has no evidence that cheating in the field of marriage reveals the character flaws that would lead to plagiarism. The writer persists:

"Bold plagiarists act like they are dying to get caught. So do bigamists. Both involve walking across a high, high wire, with no net below." That writer lacks the critical discipline to distinguish what's interesting from what's important.

If you think of focus as a sharp knife, you can test every detail in a story, and when you find something that does not fit (no matter how interesting), you can take your blade and cut it, neatly, quickly, no bleeding or suffering involved.

Ask a test reader you trust to mark the strongest and weakest elements in your story.

Even when writers are trying their best to do good work, they can easily lose perspective. It works this way: A writer has handed in a manuscript of 555 pages, even though the contract calls for 355 pages. Two hundred pages have to go, and the writer may be able to cut half of those on her own. But those last one hundred pages... Having reached a kind of mental and emotional paralysis, the writer needs a rescue.

Writers must exercise good judgment and retain some control over the people they ask to help them. Ask the wrong person, and the result may not be rescue, but burial. Too much harsh criticism can result in too much attention on weaker elements of the work without equal emphasis on the stronger.

Not long ago, I attended two one-act plays by a high school senior, Samuel French. In a conversation with the audience after the play, Sam described how he could see some elements in one of the plays that could be revised or cut. For playwrights, this process is called *workshopping*. The word suggests a social and interactive process, where the writer gets a chance to test out the material before making the next set of revisions.

Watch the DVD of a movie that contains deleted or extra scenes. Consider why particular scenes were left on the cutting-room floor.

Fans of certain movies or television shows seem endlessly fascinated by the opportunity to view deleted scenes, the stuff, according to a showbiz cliché, that is left on the cutting-room floor, a reference to older forms of film editing.

Many such lost scenes are available on YouTube, such as a half minute removed from the Lady Gaga video of her song "Paparazzi." In the comment stream, viewers debate, with surprising civility, whether the montage is worthy of inclusion. While the image of the dead French maid in the castle or of Lady Gaga sitting on a polka-dot horse are striking in and of themselves, a number of commentators could find no connection between them and the larger theme of the video.

It was fascinating to see a deleted scene from the original *Star Wars* movie between Luke Skywalker and his childhood friend Biggs Darklighter. It comes early and is all whispered talk (no action), in which Biggs reveals his plan to fly off and join the rebellion against the Empire. Luke will be stuck at home for at least another season before he gets to join the Academy. However interesting for *Star Wars* fanatics, the scene has too much gab for such an action-packed adventure, and the director found other ways to act out the background of the story.

In your reading, look for passages you might cut — even from the work of authors you admire.

One continuing benefit of working hard on the process of selection is to raise your standards as a writer and self-editor.

E. B. White was schooled at Cornell by Professor William Strunk Jr., author of the original edition of *The Elements of Style*. In more than ten million copies of the book now in print, Strunk offers this advice: "Omit needless words. Vigorous writing is concise. A sentence should contain no unnecessary words, a paragraph no unnecessary sentences, for the same reason that a drawing should have no unnecessary lines and a machine no unnecessary parts." That now famous mantra "Omit needless words" became the soul of Strunk's teaching, a strategy that turned into a habit. "In the days when I was sitting in his class," wrote White, "he omitted so many needless words, and omitted them so forcibly and with such eagerness and obvious relish, that he often seemed in the position of having shortchanged himself, a man left with nothing more to say yet with time to fill, a radio prophet who had outdistanced the clock."

As you raise standards for yourself, so you will raise them for other writers. You will become less patient with writers who prefer the modifier over the verb. You will see whole passages that prove repetitious or beside the point. The good deletions will be invisible to you unless you gain access to earlier versions. You will come to honor those who put into practice Strunk's advice that the dutiful writer should make "every word tell."

Learn from the selection strategies of other artists.

I continue to be influenced by the testimony of other artists on their methods of invention, focus, and selection. This line of inquiry began for me when I heard that jazz artist Miles Davis had described how long it took him to learn which notes to *leave out*. So creating a work of art — a novel, a screenplay, a concerto, a painting—may at first move the artist to consider what to include, but the process also demands a discipline of exclusion, the ability to make tough choices about what really matters.

Consider, for example, the work of a museum curator. Acts of curation require not just supervisory care of a collection or an exhibit, but also judgments about what to put on display, what to put on loan, and what to maintain in storage. I assume that a special Egyptian exhibition at the British Museum would include the Rosetta Stone (a discovery that helped Egyptologists decipher hieroglyphics). But which mummies should go on display? And which household artifacts?

The meaning of curation has been expanded to include the choices made by online aggregators, website editors, and bloggers. Which sites should I link to? What choices should I give my readers? Which images will be included in my slide show? We used to call such activities editing. Whatever the name, the act is one of selection.

A new music documentary called *The Promise* covers a year (1977–78) in which Bruce Springsteen and his band members created their fourth album, *Darkness on the Edge of Town,* an excruciating process of creativity and exploration that forced the Boss to exercise what he now calls his "artistic intuition" in acts of songwriting, theme making, producing, revising, and, most of all, focus and selection.

"Musically I wanted the record to sound leaner and less grand than *Born to Run,*" wrote Springsteen in 1998. "There was a lot of variation in the material we recorded, but I edited out anything I thought broke the album's tension." Every time he and the E Street Band play a concert, they apply the strategy of creative selection, choosing thirty songs to perform out of the hundreds and hundreds that they know.

—•—

Looking for Language

I am looking for a verb to describe the relationship between words and thoughts. That I cannot find one reflects the complexity of the nexus, or at least my experience of it. Sometimes it feels as if words *express* my thoughts, or *precede* my thoughts, or *follow* them, or *discover* them, or *transmit* them to others. At times the quest for words comes easy, like turning on a faucet. Then come those moments when words must be squeezed out one at a time, as from an eyedropper.

Finding the right word need not slow you down. Early drafts are by definition filled with language that is unclear, imprecise, stale, or tentative. A famous American journalist, the late Saul Pett, taught me how often the "wrong" word or metaphor is the necessary step for finding the right one. After all, for many drafts the author of *Gone with the Wind* wanted to name her heroine not Scarlett, but Pansy O'Hara.

The writer must decide on the appropriate "level" of language, a strategy that will do much to tune the author's voice. Will the language be abstract ("strategic advantage") or concrete ("a pockmarked Russian spy known only as Igor") or both? Will the allusions be to high culture (Dante's description of the divine Beatrice) or pop culture (Pee-wee Herman's description of his playhouse) or both?

Any method for finding great and appropriate language is better than staring into space and scratching your head, which is my fallback position. I often find my best words not in my brain, but out in the world. The writer conducts an interview and receives the phrase "erupted from a cracked lava lamp," or finds it in a police report, or sees it in a magazine ad, or captures it from direct observation. I read dictionaries for fun. I read phone books to stumble upon interesting names (just found Drago Stamen). I am never shy about seeing something new and asking the expert, "What do you call that?" or "Does that thingy have a name?"

Problems covered in this chapter:

TOO FEW WORDS

Just because you cannot find the words does not mean you have nothing to say. In fact, you may not need as many words as you think to make your case. A 500-word essay—if each word were different—would only require 500 words, a tiny portion of both your reading and writing vocabularies. Shakespeare used as many as 25,000 words—but those were counted from 33 five-act plays and more than 150 separate poems. His rivals, including writers such as Marlowe and Jonson, achieved canonical status with a vocabulary only half as large as the Bard's.

The key is to find the right word, the best word for a particular job in the available time. Finding that word requires two strategies, one that takes a lifetime and one less than a day. Over the years, from your childhood on, it is the quality and quantity of your reading that enriches your vocabulary, along with application of the basic tools of lexicography: the dictionary and the thesaurus. But your ability to find the right word *today* depends not on owning a deep treasure chest full of words, but on your ability to gather words as part of your reporting and research.

Every group, every place, every family, has its own hoard of words that sets it apart. Language scholars call this a "discourse community." The writer has to ask the mechanic: "What do you call that?" "That, my friend, is a timing belt, and if it frays and then snaps while you are driving eighty miles an hour on the Interstate, you, my friend, are screwed." Look at the marvelous language unleashed by my question: I get verbs such as *frays* and *snaps;* a technical term: *timing belt;* and a bit of irreverent slang: *screwed.*

TIRED AND STALE

George Orwell advised writers to avoid phrases and images they were used to seeing in print. Playing your cards close to the vest...getting the lay of the land...minding your p's and q's...facing the music...toeing the line...putting your nose to the grindstone...swimming against the tide...Whoever used these phrases first created something fresh, but they have become stale from overuse.

Many sources for stories think and speak in clichés, so it becomes the job of the writer to ask questions that take a source deeper, or at least to the point where the language begins to sound distinctive and original. The hockey player may say, "We knew it was a do-or-die situation," or "We've had our backs against the wall before." What I would prefer is "I figured that cleaning my golf clubs could wait another day," that is, for the off-season after the championship victory.

The occasional colorful phrase, even if it's a cliché, is not a problem. The problem comes when the clichés multiply and take over the story like text-eating bacteria. A mosaic of clichés is a form of automatic thinking. The writer may write such a draft, which makes revision all the more important. Give yourself a chance to think of something original, or at least plain, to replace the hackneyed language that clip-clopped into your text.

CLOUDY LANGUAGE

Although clarity is often extolled as a great effect of purposeful prose, it is not a universal value. I would not describe "The Wasteland" by poet T. S. Eliot as "clear." The language of government, law, and diplomacy can be intentionally ambiguous, leaving a text open to various interpretations. Works of philosophy, theology, and cosmology can have many excellent qualities; clarity is not always one of them.

Writers who serve a general audience must avoid the trap of describing complex issues in complicated prose. The writers who turn hard facts into easy reading understand that shorter and simpler are often better at the points of greatest density or complexity. Their best explanations make the writing look deceptively easy, going down like lemonade on a hot Florida day.

Plain English, it turns out, is the product of craft: an understanding of the reader's needs, the translation of alienating jargon, establishing an easy pace that readers can follow. Clarity of expression comes most of all from a clear understanding of the topic or theme you are writing about. No writer can clarify for the reader what is not clear to the writer in the first place.

REFLECT

- Do you like to play with words for professional or personal reasons?
- What do you do when you come across an unfamiliar word?
- Can you think of a time when someone expressed surprise at your use of a particular word?
- Are you afraid of using new or unusual words for fear that readers will not understand them?
- Have you ever invented a word or adapted an old word for a new purpose?
- Write down adjectives (*plain, muscular, brainy*) that describe your authentic writing voice. Now reread an old story of yours (a good one) to see the language choices you used to create that specific effect.
- It has been said that there are no true synonyms. Does that ring true? (Consider, for example, *rock/stone, sofa/couch, naked/nude.*)
- In a journal or notebook, keep a list of interesting words or phrases that you encounter in your reading, writing, and conversation.

10

My vocabulary is so limited.

If you can't find the words, let the words find you.

During the gathering stage of writing, you'll include a hunt for language. A good vocabulary comes from many sources, but especially from habitual reading—deep and wide—on topics both big and small. In the short run, a richer vocabulary often comes from research.

An old paradigm of writing and language never worked for me. I can't write by sitting in one place, looking to the sky for inspiration, asking my muse for words to make a story or essay. Instead, I've got to light out for the territory and find not just information, facts, and details, but, just as important, language.

Yesterday I wrote a brief opinion piece on the new president of a local college, a man I contrasted to his predecessor, whom I described as *pharaonic*. My spell-checker did not recognize the word and suggested that I might have meant *paranoiac, harmonic,* or *parabolic.* But no, I meant pharaonic, which means "in the style of an Egyptian pharaoh."

Where did that word come from? It came from gathering information on the former president, who, over three decades, built many buildings on several new campuses, "pyramids of learning," I called them. The word *pyramid* led me to the word *pharaoh,* which led me to *pharaonic.* That word led to two others, the name Ramses II, one of the great ancient Egyptian pyramid builders, and to that of his foil, Moses, which allowed me to describe the new president as being more Mosaic than pharaonic. As you can see, the first word, *pyramid,* came from gathering and the others flowed easily by association.

Create a lexicon for each of the topics you write about.

A lexicographer is someone who creates lists of words, as in a dictionary. At one time or another, all writers become amateur word trackers. The reason is simple. Writers like to write about people, especially groups of people: lumberjacks, pole dancers, astrophysicists, plumbers, kindergarten teachers. The members of those groups communicate with one another in specialized languages that bond them into a community and create guarded gates of language to keep others out.

Let's take one of the world's most popular entertainment enterprises, professional wrestling. This combination of morality play and acrobat circus has heroes and villains, but that's not what they are called. For generations, the bad guys have been known as "heels," and the good guys as "faces," short for "baby faces." Many wrestlers need a "gimmick," some strange costume or prop, as when Brutus "the Barber" Beefcake carried a pair of scissors into the ring to clip his opponent's locks after a victory. When they enter the arena, the most popular figures get a loud response—boos or cheers—called a "pop" from the crowd.

When the group you are covering has professional status, we call their specialized language "jargon"; for example, the way people in government use "funding" instead of the more common "money." When the group is outcast or marginalized, such as prostitutes or pornographers, we refer to their tribal language as "slang." A male porn star who can't perform is said to have "wood trouble," sometimes requiring the assistance of a "fluffer," whose job it is to get him back in working order. Who knew that lexicography could be such fun?

Keep in mind the "discourse community" or language club you are writing for.

The language or diction you use in a story depends on your sense of audience. Each of us owns a spice rack full of language styles to satisfy the appetites of the different language communities we serve as writers. The members of my Catholic parish, St. Paul's, form one discourse community; the newsroom of the *St. Pete Times* another; the morning crowd at Banyan restaurant another.

If I am writing for the church bulletin, I might use "transubstantiation" and "Fall Carnival" in the same message. In the newsroom, you might hear me talking about "attribution," "computer-assisted reporting," or "getting the name of the dog." At the breakfast bar, a character named Go Go may shout friendly profanity at a lawyer nicknamed Rooster, while Flo orders a "half-caf cappuccino." Different wards, different words, a habit that linguists describe as "code switching."

Your close attention to a person or a place will find you the language you need, but you should choose your specific words with the needs of readers in mind. This may mean getting to know your audience as a discourse community, not to kowtow to its language preferences but to keep comprehensibility high on your list of effects.

Ask your sources for the names of things.

What do you call that thing I can attach to my laptop to back up my files?

Oh, that's a flash drive.

What do you call the first three community cards in Texas hold 'em poker?

That's called the "flop," the next card is the "turn," the last card is the "river."

Professor, what was that long word you used to describe the philosophy of how we know things? It sounded like it had "piss" in it.

Yeah, but with only one *s:* "epistemology."

What do you call that amazing move when the soccer player turns his back to the goal and then kicks the ball back over his head?

You mean a "bicycle kick"?

What do you call that piano technique when you finish one chord progression and start a new one?

I think you mean a "turnaround."

What do you call that little punching bag in the back of the throat?

That's called the "uvula," from the Latin word for "swollen grape."

You get the idea. One of the writer's most powerful questions is "What do you call that thing?"

To give yourself time to notice, go early and stay late.

Showing up at an event early and staying late lets you scout out the most revealing knickknacks and artifacts, story details that will yield, along with the power of particularity, some interesting language. I am standing just outside the office pod of one of my young colleagues, Ellyn Angelotti. If I were writing a profile of her, I'd have the benefit of a subject with a lilting Italian surname that means "little angel," so I'd have scored already.

Now I'm looking at her display case filled with an array of personal items and decorative memorabilia. I'm writing in my notebook the name of any object I recognize, or the name or brand marked on each. In three minutes, I have completed this inventory:

- A lava lamp
- A stuffed purple porpoise
- Pink Mardi Gras beads
- Three games: Kerplunk!, Hangman, and Jenga
- A cup with the name Data Glyphics
- A Kansas University plaque with its sports cheer: Rock Chalk Jayhawk
- A tiny waving hula dancer with the word *Aloha* on the base

Look at the treasure trove of language unlocked by three minutes of close observation: lava lamp, Kerplunk!, purple porpoise, aloha, Mardi Gras...Without having to come up with a single word, we have not only visual details we can use in a story, but made-to-order alliteration, onomatopoeia, and a taste of Hawaiian and French.

Keep track of key words in your reading.

A former English major, I harbor an apprehension about the worlds of science and math, which is why, as I described earlier, I compensate for my insecurities with my reading. I always have a book nearby that unlocks for me the ways in which scientists understand the world. As I read, I learn a lot of new words, and some old words used in new ways.

An article on embryonic stem cell research introduced me to language such as "a procedure called somatic-cell nuclear transfer." Then "chemicals coax the doctored egg to reproduce itself," forming a "cluster" of cells called a "blastocyst." That single passage gives me access to some scientific terms, especially "blastocyst," which would be a blast to use in a sentence. But it also gives me the clever wordplay of a "doctored egg," with all its splendid connotations. I will make a note of these in my daybook so I can revisit them and harvest the best for my own use.

William T. Vollmann wrote a book called *Uncentering the Earth: Copernicus and The Revolutions of the Heavenly Spheres.* That may be one of the best titles in the history of narrative nonfiction. The word *revolutions* gives us an image of planets revolving around suns, but also refers to the scientific paradigm shifts that helped us reimagine the universe. *Uncentering* is a brilliant word, denoting the removal of the earth from its central place in the Great Chain of Being, but also referring to the confusion, controversy, and instability caused by scientific challenges to a theological vision of the cosmos. I now own the word *uncentering* and predict I will use it down the road.

Explode old words for new meaning.

"Where does that word come from?"

"Let's look it up."

Those two sentences will enrich your vocabulary and offer new pathways of research.

Many words have long histories going back millennia to the Indo-European roots of our culture, and the study of the history of words is well documented and available to all writers. That study is called *etymology*, not to be confused with *entomology*, the study of bugs. I have no idea where those words came from (it all looks Greek to me), so I will look them up.

OK, I now know that the ancient Greek word *etumon* denotes the "true sense" of a word. So my guess is that the prefix *entomo-* has something to do with insects. Give me a moment....OK, I found a surprise here. It does come from a Greek word for insect, but that word derives from a word that means "to cut up," a reference to the segmented bodies of insects.

When Don Fry and I were writing a book for editors titled *Coaching Writers,* I asked Don, "Why do you think the word *coach* has two meanings? We have Cinderella's coach, but we also have basketball coach Bobby Knight." Predictably Don said, "Let's look it up in the *Oxford English Dictionary!*"

The coach you ride in, it turns out, is named after a city in Hungary where they were manufactured (the Motown of the sixteenth century). The sense of *coach* as athletic trainer comes much later, in the universities of Victorian England. The origins are not clear, but we speculated that the English coach, a tutor who prepared students for their exams, was the metaphoric "vehicle" to help transport students toward the learning they needed to acquire.

Finding the history of one word will also remind you of words that are connected to the same root, such as *famine/famish* or *venereal/venerate/venerable/Venus.* Look it up. Learn. Watch the word explode. Pick up the pieces of meaning.

Learn the relationship between your reading and writing vocabularies.

Unless we are impaired, we all work from four sets of vocabularies, two that are receptive and two that are expressive. The largest of these is your reading vocabulary, which comprises the others: listening, speaking, and writing. Shakespeare, remember, had a writing vocabulary of about 25,000 words, twice as large as that of other writers of his time, five times larger than the average person's reading vocabulary. In fact, if a person knows the thousand most common words, that person can read more than two-thirds of most of the texts she will ever encounter.

How does this help you as a writer? Chances are, most of your readers have reading vocabularies bigger than your writing vocabulary. You may be censoring yourself in an effort to achieve maximum comprehensibility. Though you may be tempted to write *eleemosynary,* you'll fall back on *charitable.*

I see from a quick check of the dictionary that the word *languid* (meaning "lacking energy or vitality") is in my reading vocabulary, but I can't remember ever using it in my writing. Nor have I used, or do I understand, the word just above it: *languet,* which means "shaped like a tongue," as in "the languet petals of the flower."

Most of my readers would probably not understand either word without a clear context or accompanying definition. But what about these words (I am about to open my dictionary to a random page): *gelatin, geisha, Geiger counter, gecko, gee whiz.* These, I would argue, are in range for most readers. I have no memory of ever having used these words in a story (unlike *geek* and *geezer*), even though they have been waiting for a long time in my reading vocabulary.

Get the name of the dog.

To enliven your prose, it helps to compile a list of proper names that are relevant to your story. In St. Pete, our shorthand command for this type of detail is "Get the name of the dog." But it can also be the name of the bread (Wonder). Or the name of the car (Mustang). Or the brand of the cigarette (Camel) or beer (Keystone).

If you write fiction, poetry, or drama you will be inventing names. The nonfiction writer, of course, collects, rather than invents, and in many cases the novelist collects in order to inspire creative invention. For your novel or play, open your local telephone directory at random, as I am about to do. You will, I predict, be amazed at the diversity, beauty, quirkiness of the names you'll encounter, seeds for names you can invent. On page 148, I found these beauties: James Glinka, J. A. Glock, Frank Glore, Stan and Vicki Glow, L. Glunt, Gus Glyptis, Joseph Gnozzo, Glen Gobervilla, Mark Godcharles, Betty

Goebel, John Gogay, Paul Going. All those beautiful G names sharing a single page.

If you are covering the fire at a kennel, your prose will be enriched by learning the names of the dogs that were rescued: Scooch, Honeybun, Trixie, Bluto, Rusty, Lulu, Mandrake, Rush, Zee Baby, Orion, Buckshot, Lancelot, and Rex. Now that you know them, you have the opportunity to play with the order of those names for maximum effect.

Don't just describe that "thingy," name it.

I once wrote an essay in which I described those final stages of revision when you take all the commas out, then put them back in, or dump a word, replace it, dump the second word for a third, then go back to the first. My point was that it becomes harder and harder to determine whether those finishing touches really make the story better.

I was looking for an analogy and came up with one from the field of ophthalmology. From the time I was a terribly near-sighted ten year old to getting lens implants after cataract surgery, I've spent hundreds of hours sitting in the chair at the eye doctor. During those examinations, the doc often swings this big machine over your face, turns out the lights, and tests your vision. The doctor tries this lens and that lens until your vision gets sharper. As you get closer to the end of the exam, it becomes harder to distinguish the effect of a particular lens. "Which is better," asks the doctor, "A or B? Let me do it again. A or B? A little better?" "No," I respond, "a little worse."

That's it! Writers need the equivalent of that machine, that eye-thingy, to fine-tune their work. Eye-thingy? I called Dr. Updegraff's office and described the machine to a nurse. "Oh, that's a phoropter," I learned. My spell-check wanted me to change it to *chiropter* or *promoter,* and I couldn't find it in my two favorite dictionaries. But a quick Google search did the trick, not only verifying *phoropter,* but offering a photo. I've used that word since in several practical contexts in both my writing and teaching, but I would never have been able to marshal it metaphorically had I not reached out and discovered its name.

11

—•—

My early drafts are littered with clichés.

Don't worry about the occasional cliché.

Clichés would not exist if they were not useful and memorable. The problem occurs when formulaic language becomes a substitute for thinking. The word *cliché*, from the French, has an interesting origin: *The American Heritage Dictionary* describes it as a word that imitates the sound of an old printing machine. (The word *stereotype* also comes from printing.) The sense is that as the printer stamps out identical texts, so the mechanical writer bangs out prefabricated bits of prose.

Since everything that is not eternal must begin at some specific time and place, it is logical to assume that clichés were once fresh and original, a quality that led to their being imitated. It is that replication of language that turns something distinctive into something predictable.

I know writers and teachers who say they want to ban clichés from their own work and the work of others. Not only is the effort futile, it's counterproductive. Not all clichés are created equal (is "created equal" a cliché?). Some, though recognizable, are picturesque and retain the ability to delight—at least in certain contexts. Two of my favorites are "the fleas come with the dog" and "whistling past the graveyard."

Consider these pieces of dialogue for context:

"He is so brilliant. But I hate it when he thinks he's always right."

"Hey, the fleas come with the dog!" (In other words, it's inevitable that something annoying would accompany something that is otherwise excellent.)

"And he seems so optimistic about the future of the business."

"That's just Gary whistling past the graveyard." (In other words, trying his best to hide his mortal anxiety with a casual air.)

So choose your clichés as you would other elements of language. Select the most interesting and appropriate phrase, and use it to create a specific effect.

Recognize when you are using clichés in clusters.

Orwell encouraged writers to create original images instead of the standard clichés, slogans, and euphemisms of political propaganda. That's hard to do, but worth the effort. His concern, he argued in "Politics and the English Language," was that the flesh-and-blood writer could transform into an ideological automaton:

When one watches some tired hack...repeating the familiar phrases...one often has a curious feeling that one is not watching a live human being but some kind of dummy: a feeling which suddenly becomes stronger at moments when the light catches the speaker's spectacles and turns them into blank discs which seem to have no eyes behind them. And this is not altogether fanciful. A speaker who uses that kind of phraseology has gone some distance towards turning himself into a machine.

Such ideological sloganeering can be seen to this day, perhaps more persistently in America, where political campaigns are long and television advertising is pervasive. So who is this new candidate for governor of Florida? You can write the ad yourself. He is a "workingman" who comes from a "good family" and who does not want to practice "politics as usual." He is suspicious of the "special interests" and the "career politicians in Tallahassee," one of whom he will never become until, of course, he becomes one.

One cliché per story, report, or essay is a good number. One in every two stories is better.

Don't be afraid to take a cliché and tweak it.

A bit of improvisation can take a stale phrase and bring it back refreshed. The fleece of a lamb is rarely pure white, which could lead to: "...its fleece was white as New York snow." Consider, for example, this poem "My Makeup," by Rochelle Kraut:

on my cheeks I wear
the flush of two beers

on my eyes I use
the dark circles of sleepless nights
to great advantage

for lipstick
I wear my lips

While the "flush of two beers" takes common words and weaves an original image, the phrases "dark circles" and "sleepless nights" verge on the clichéd, until we learn those circles are not covered by her makeup, they *are* her makeup.

Dorothy Parker is among the popular writers who gained fame by her ability to knock out a familiar phrase with a punch line at the end: "You can lead a horse to water, but you can't make him drink" became "You can lead a horticulture, but you can't make her think." "One more drink and I'll be under the table" became "One more drink and I'll be under the host."

Through years of economic growth, I'd hear the bullish prediction that "A rising tide lifts all boats." Since the recession of 2008, I've found myself repeating a contrarian mantra: "All boats sink on a low tide." Though this is not literally true, my new phrase gains strength by tweaking the nose of conventional wisdom.

When tempted by a cliché, give yourself one minute to think of an alternative.

Write the cliché ("old hat") on a piece of paper and list words or phrases that come close to the same meaning.

- That idea is too old.
- That new idea is not new.

- That idea has already been tried.
- That idea has been stored in mothballs.
- That idea is in cold storage.
- That idea is like a bug captured in amber.
- That idea is made of straw.
- That idea is tired.
- That's not brainstorming; it's brain numbing.
- Did you find that in an antique-clothing store?

Some of these, I recognize, hit the target, and others miss the mark. No matter. You will need examples that do not work in order to find one that illuminates your meaning in an original way. And remember, you can always use "old hat" if you can't find anything better.

Be cautious of the "buzzword," the instant cliché spun off by the culture.

Buzzwords are instant clichés that elbow their way into business meetings and PowerPoint presentations. They sound important but do not stand up as anything more than jargon. *The American Heritage Dictionary* defines a buzzword as "a word or phrase connected with a specialized field or group that usually sounds important or technical and is used primarily to impress laypersons." A second meaning is "a stylish or trendy word or phrase." Notice that these two meanings are in some tension. The first meaning denotes language generated by a specialized group to impress outsiders; the second suggests a word that has public excitement around it like a buzz.

Think of the first meaning as jargon, as when managers refer to "efficiency downsizing" when they mean "saving money by firing workers." Think of the second meaning as a form of slang that busts out from a special group into the general population, like referring to jewelry as "bling."

"The language of business," writes Ruth Cullen in her lexicon *The Little Hiptionary,* "is a curious combination of bureaucratic jargon, ungrammatical posturing, and locker room lingo." In my time, we "gravitated" to "synergy," "perfect storms," and "pushing the envelope." Cullen records "deliverables" (work products), "crackberry" (a person addicted to his mobile phone), "cube farm" (offices made up of cubicles), and "granular" (detailed down to the grain). Suddenly everyone in the culture is "shifting paradigms" and "peeling the onion," only to find themselves "out of the loop." The writer can have fun disinfecting such language in the public interest.

Write down the cliché and begin to improvise off it.

White as snow. White as a sheet. White as New York snow. White as cocaine. White as a Klansman. Black as a Klansman's heart. White as a thundercloud.

Brown as a berry. Brown as a burnt berry. Brown as a blueberry (not brown at all). Brown as Bob Berry (tanning champion). Brown as a pair of brown shoes worn with a tuxedo.

Green as grass. Green as marijuana. Green as jealous grass. Green as a ten-year-old boy chewin' on his first wad of tobacco.

Blue as the sky. Blue as dusk. Blue as a broken heart. Blue as B.B. King.

Clear as day. Clear as night. Clear as sweet iced tea. Clear as a letter from the IRS.

It's not rocket science. It *is* rocket science. It's not rocket science…it's *harder* than rocket science. What's so hard about rocket science?

Make sure you understand the origin of the cliché. It's "toe the line" not "tow the line."

People think it's "tow the line," like pulling a heavy weight with a rope. But it's "toe the line," from old boxing rules requiring a struggling fighter to step up to a line drawn in the dirt, demonstrating his ability to continue battle.

I thought until recently that the phrase was "to soft-peddle" the proposal, that is to offer or sell it softly. Someone else thought it was "to soft-pedal," which is correct, but mistakenly thought it derived from bicycle racing. It was only while playing the piano that I remembered that it comes with at least two pedals, a "loud" one to sustain the sound and a "soft pedal" to mute it.

Some clichés have such a twisted history they may have become useless. As an urban/suburban boy, I had no notion of what it meant to have "a long row to hoe." I heard it as "a long road to hold," which I imagined to be derived from the world of race car driving. I expect to hear a rap song someday about it being a "long road for a ho." The reference all you farm writers will recognize is to the physical labor that comes from using a hoe to cultivate a row of crops.

Some etymologies derived from myth or folklore can confuse the writer and the reader. If you have any doubts as to whether you are using a cliché correctly, check out its origins, and even if it fits with your meaning, give yourself a chance to think of something original.

Conduct an Internet search on your cliché. Perhaps it is not as overused as you think — or more overused.

There's no magic metric to test the freshness of a phrase, but a search engine can lead you to thousands, even millions of examples of a phrase's usage and misusage. Responsible writers want their work to be original. They don't want to snatch the work of others, even if only a catchy phrase. We all suffer from what critic Harold Bloom once described as "the anxiety of influence."

It has been proven time and again that writers working independently can come up with the same or similar expressions to describe an event or phenomenon. When the Salvador Dalí Museum opened in St. Petersburg, I expected clever headline writers and columnists to consider "Hello, Dalí" as one of their options. The problem comes with what I call "first-level creativity," the result of the glib-erati all inventing the same bon mots at the same time. Who wants to be the seventeenth writer to invent that "apt phrase"?

In fact, let's see what a Google search comes up with for "apt phrase." In typical fashion, in less than a second, the search turns up 118,000 links for "apt phrase," and a quick review of the first hundred or so sources reveals a rich variety of applications, perhaps turning it into an "app phrase." Nobody owns the phrase, even in references to possible plagiarism cases, and the number of links is small compared to the number of links to other obvious clichés. So the phrase appears to be fair game for writers.

Oops, better look up "fair game."

Be sensitive to clichés of language, but even more to clichés of vision, tired ways of seeing the world.

I learned the phrase "clichés of vision" from Donald Murray's classic book *Writing to Deadline*. While clichés of language may be misdemeanors, clichés of vision are felonies, a failure to see the world in all its complexities. Among those stereotypes of vision, Murray includes:

- The victim is always innocent.
- Corporate executives are workaholics.
- Bureaucrats are lazy.
- Housewives hate being housewives.
- Politicians are crooked.
- Gays cruise.
- It's lonely at the top.
- It's boring in the suburbs.
- It's exciting in the city.

It was my neighbor Jack Leonard who taught me most about clichés of vision and how they blur the ability of the writer to see things straight. Jack was a quadriplegic when I met him, the victim of a waterskiing accident in his youth. Because he lived a productive and gallant life until his death more than thirty years after the accident, many writers discovered him and profiled his achievements. Jack would always laugh at them for not seeing the real story. To him, the real story involved his wife, Jackie. When Jack was injured, he and Jackie already had a baby and she was pregnant with another. Jack was helpless without her. She was responsible for getting him up each morning, getting his food into a form he could eat, seeing to the equipment that supported him. "It's always about the 'heroic' cripple," Jack would say, and never about the caregiver without whose love and attention he could not have survived a single day.

Cautiously avoid ideological sloganeering.

Our political discourse has devolved into a war of slogans from the left and the right, a form of propaganda that reduces complicated issues to simple messages designed to stir emotions rather than appeal to reason. On the most contentious issues, each side battles not just for ideas or policies, but for the language that will give them the high ground.

For abortion it's the child versus the fetus, life versus choice. For immigration it's protecting our borders versus being the land of immigrants, undocumented workers versus illegal aliens. In matters of actual war, one side tells us that "freedom is on the march" and that the other side wants to "cut and run." One candidate declares himself the candidate of "change," forcing his opponent to become the candidate of "real change." (I look forward to the day when a panhandler declares himself the candidate of "spare change.")

These language choices are not automatic or arbitrary. They are the products of those within the political system who want to sell an idea or a candidate, usually for a narrow interest. The writer must be alert to such abuses of language, call attention to them, and avoid them in his own work.

12

—•—

My words don't make things clear.

Translate jargon for the reader.

Technical language gives power to some and keeps it from others. Translating jargon lets readers in on the secret. The powerful may not approve. Plain-language bills in state legislatures sometimes run into trouble with lawyers who fear that enlightened amateurs will steal their business. The Protestant Reformation included efforts to translate the Bible into the vernacular, breaking bonds with clerics who controlled interpretations of Latin texts.

In that sense, good writers are translators of a language that may be English but which can sound foreign to the civilian ear. "More than anything, a journalist is an explainer of complicated issues," wrote CBS's Fred Friendly in his foreword to

Writing News for Broadcast by Edward Bliss. "Before he can explain, he must understand. Before he can understand, he must search. And before he can do that, he must be predisposed to examine with equal parity facts and personalities he dislikes, as well as those he may support."

A champion of jargon-less language was Robert Gunning, who coached writers from many different businesses on how to take the fog out of their prose. A great first step, argued Gunning, was to simplify words and phrases that may have been inflated to create the impression that the document is more highfalutin than it is. *Accumulate* becomes *gather; ameliorate* becomes *improve; approximately* becomes *about; assistance* becomes *aid.* And those are just the A's!

Here's what good writing looks like when the jargon is translated (from Timothy Ferris, *The Whole Shebang*):

> Describing it [the big bang] requires that we define a few terms. The big bang theory holds that the universe began in a *singularity*—a state of infinite curvature of spacetime. In a singularity, all places and times are the same. Hence the big bang did not take place in a preexisting space; all space was embroiled *in* the big bang. Nor did the big bang happen in a remote location: It happened right where you are, and everywhere else. All places that exist today were originally the same place.

Such writing eliminates all barriers to entry. "Step right up," says the author like a carnival barker, "and see the cosmos dance."

Use as few numbers as possible and place them in context.

If you must use numbers, limit them. If possible, use just one number. If more are required, spread them out so they don't bump into one another. I've encountered a different strategy: that you should group key numbers so that the reader can deal with them and move forward. For me, when I see a block of numbers, I'm inclined to skip them, assuming that the significance of those numbers will be explained down in the story.

William Blundell, a veteran of the *Wall Street Journal,* a publication not afraid of numbers, once revealed that his best stories had no numbers in them. "We know that too many numbers are poison, so the writer's first impulse should be to omit unessential ones," he wrote in *The Art and Craft of Feature Writing.*

> The good writer also recasts as many numbers as he can in a simpler or more pictorial form that removes some of their abstraction. If a precise figure is not important, he rounds it off: $2.6 million is cleaner and easier than $2,611,423. If something increased by 36.7%, he may say it went up more than a third. If it increased by 98%, he says it almost doubled. These expressions are pictorial in that they let the reader visualize a slice of a pie or two pies where there was one before.

Lift the heaviest information into a chart or graph.

There is a better way to make numbers more pictorial: Draw a picture. For years now, Mario Garcia, the world's most influential media designer, has preached to writers and editors the value of "lifting the heavy cargo of the story" out of the text and into a visual element. This can be done with a pie chart or a fever graph (a chart that looks like a fever thermometer) or a locator map or dozens of other standard strategies of visual expression. If you are trying to demonstrate that the winner of the big poker tournament took home a lot of money, you can say $5 million, but you could also use a photograph of him holding the winner's bracelet over a huge pile of cash spread across the table.

Although writers need not know how to assemble survey information into visual form, you are wise to understand the value of such a strategy. With a collaborative mind-set, you can provide a graphic artist the necessary statistical information to do the job as early in the process as possible, not as an afterthought. I have learned how to talk with artists and designers without an accent, making sure they feel like partners in the creative process of informing the public.

Another value of using visuals involves the power of repetition. Blundell advises writers that if they have something important to say, they should say it over and over again but in different forms: in a number, in a caption, in the text, in an illustration.

Slow down the pace of information.

Never pack information into sentences or paragraphs, a strategy sometimes derided as "suitcasing." If your suitcase is overpacked, it may not close, so you'll sit on it until it does. The ill consequences of such a strategy may be nothing more than wrinkled clothes or, at worst, a fee at the airport for a bag that's too heavy.

When you write in suitcase style, however, the consequences can be more significant, especially when the packing of facts, numbers, acronyms, and technical language results in text so dense it defies all attempts to comprehend the writer's main point.

To make complexity comprehensible, the writer must slow down the pace for the reader:

> The City Council approved a lean new budget Thursday, cutting more that 10% from last year's budget and adding a mil (one tenth of one percent) to the tax rate of homeowners.

The reader's got a little work to do to grasp this information, but compared to the worst examples of cluttered writing, this works reasonably well. We know that the budget is lean (a pictorial metaphor), that budget cutting would save money, and that property taxes would raise money. Notice in my paraphrase that I avoid the technical word *mil* and use no numbers at all. Important numbers could always be highlighted in a chart or graph.

If you've ever struggled in a math or science class, you know what it means for the information to be moving too fast. The good teacher will not let students lag but will slow the pace of learning so that they can catch up. In the same sense, readers learn best at a slower pace: one difficult bit at a time.

Use shorter words, shorter sentences, shorter paragraphs at the points of greatest complexity.

This must be among the handful of most useful strategies passed down to writers by Donald Murray. When I first heard this golden advice, it seemed contrarian, violating the notion that form must follow function. If something is complex — the collapse of the housing market — we might be inclined to think that the text explaining it should be complex as well.

The true solution rubs against that grain. Shorter sentences mean more periods. More periods mean more stopping points. More stopping points create a slower pace for the reader. A slower pace helps the reader digest bits and bites. I'm exaggerating the effect in this paragraph, which is getting tedious from too many sentences of the same length. But the idea is sound: smaller units of language at the points of greatest complexity.

When I struggle with this problem, I often revert to a sentence that pushes me onto the right path: "Here's how it works...." Those four words — either in my head or on the page — lead me to language that is plain vanilla, coaxing me to adopt the words of a teacher or tour guide rather than a scholar or technical expert.

Focus on the impact.

A famous editor once told his city hall reporter that he wanted more city and less hall. Readers will engage with a piece of writing if they know it's written with their needs in mind. My first city editor, Mike Foley, taught me to avoid writing reports that said in effect, "They held a meeting Thursday." The meeting itself was not important, argued Foley. Did they raise property taxes? If so, the writer has a duty to convey the consequences to the reader. If necessary, the writer might teach readers how to compute property taxes based on the value of their property and the new rate of taxation.

It should not surprise us that the biggest stories have the

biggest impact, often too large to calculate. What was the impact of World War II on the Allies? No one on earth is qualified to measure it. Where would we start? Number of dead and wounded? The cost of replacing cities destroyed by bombs? The trauma of refugee displacement?

As I write this sentence, the United States government has taken over control of trying to fix the largest oil spill in history, which is spreading every day across the Gulf of Mexico. The story has a technical dimension, to be sure: What went wrong? How will it be fixed? What can be done so it never happens again? The writing will be clearer and more compelling if we are able to see the human impact: not just the eleven workers killed on the oil rig explosion, but also an unknown future and the loss of wetlands, fisheries, and the jobs of those whose livelihood comes from the sea. I'm looking for a bird rescuer washing the oil from pelican wings with dish soap, or for an abandoned business along a polluted beach, or for a shrimper trying to pull in one more boatload before the toxic oil creeps in.

Alternate between what is important and what is interesting.

I've already insisted that the writer's duty is to make important things interesting to the reader. Important stuff — if tedious — will drive readers away. So spice up those Brussels sprouts. This mode is nothing like the one practiced by celebrity or tabloid writers who make things that can be quite interesting — a popular actor going into rehab — seem important, blowing up the coverage beyond all proportionality.

Serious writers have a problem and an opportunity when they find their notebooks and files filled with both interesting and important material, though the interesting stuff may not be so important, and the important stuff not so interesting. Consider this short list of actual details from a local news story:

- Man watches gator slither into a ditch not far from trailer park.
- He calls team of firefighters stationed nearby.
- Man falls into ditch headfirst.
- Firefighters play tug-of-war with gator to get man out.
- Man sustains wound on arm that requires fifty stitches.
- Special crew is called to capture gator.
- They pull him up, and gathering crowd oohs and ahhs.
- Ten-foot gator is taken away to be "euthanized."

These bare details reveal a real-life narrative that may not require much elaboration. But editors and readers will seize on serious questions for Floridians such as: Where did the gator come from? What should you do if you see a gator near a trailer park or in your backyard? Should all such gators be killed even if contact is the fault of humans? The writer has the choice to answer these questions in a single story block or to spread them out, balancing the scales between interesting and important.

Have a chat with your imaginary friend.

My brother Vincent, now a professional actor, had a funny habit as a kid. Alone in his room, he could constantly be heard talking in different voices. But to whom? We called this phantom "Vinnie's friend," and now realize he was just rehearsing for a wonderful acting career. Turns out, an imaginary friend can be quite useful. (Take that, Mom!)

You may be mired in complexity. A single conversation with a single person can force you to simplify your message. Don't be fussy. This can work as an actual face-to-face conversation, an exchange of messages, or a chat with a make-believe friend. Writers have confessed to me that they imagine a conversation on the phone with someone they know or a chat with a friendly stranger on the next bar stool.

What is complex in your head can become clearer by the simple act of translating thought into language, oral or written. You may get a good question in return, or some feedback. But you may not need it. Your monologue might sound something like this:

"OK. I'm writing about something very complicated, which I am trying to understand myself. It has to do with how a motion picture company went from a year of loss to a year of profit. What interests me most is what did *not* happen. The company did not make better movies that brought in more revenue. In fact, they did only one thing: They hired a new group of accountants. They fired the ones who calculated that they were in the red; the new ones—using a special accounting method—looked at the same data but were able to come up with a more favorable conclusion."

Such an utterance has multiple benefits: (1) It helps the writer know whether she really understands; (2) it helps the editor or teacher know whether the writer is on the right track; (3) it creates opportunities for questions and suggestions.

Make the strange feel familiar.

Although fiction writers may strive to make the familiar feel strange, it is the job of the explanatory writer to make the strange feel familiar. Tools such as analogies and metaphors help readers understand something new in terms of what they already know. A curious friend would certainly be able to make sense of author Jack Fuller's prose in *What Is Happening to News,* even though the content is theoretical.

> Natural selection explains a great deal about why our brains came to have the structure they have today. It may be helpful to think of natural selection as a kind of tinkering. It does not build a structural feature that fits a particular purpose or ecological niche by starting from scratch. Instead, it takes what already exists and works from there. That is why our bodies contain features that trace directly back to quite differently functioning structures in earlier species. Or, as evolutionary biologist Neil Shubin cleverly put it, if we look hard enough into our own bodies, we can find our "inner fish."

The simple clarity of such prose may mask its true genius. It takes a brainy and curious writer to figure out what a technical concept means, and a skillful writer to render it for a general audience. What is sometimes called the "plain style" may look effortless, but it takes a rigorous execution of craft, beginning with learning the key words, translating them from words of Latin and Greek origin to straight English, and finding an elegant analogy that makes the mysterious somehow familiar.

Keep the dullest parts short.

I keep next to my computer an old saying attributed to an influential editor named Barney Kilgore: "The easiest thing for a reader to do is to quit reading." A corollary might go like this: "The reader will forgive the writer for almost anything—but not for being a bore."

The best way to deal with some difficult information is to leave it out of the story. Or edit it from a draft through revision. It may seem odd, but readers may understand more if writers give them less. To do this responsibly, an author must make tough value judgments on the information collected, a selectivity that produces a more precise, more readable story.

Although I know of no reliable calculus on how much boring stuff the reader will tolerate, a good test begins with your own behaviors and sensibilities as a reader. Look at your bookshelf for works that you began reading but then stopped. Perhaps you can find the exact place where you put that novel or biography aside. As a reader—and thus as a writer—I have a three-paragraph standard: Something must raise my interest every three paragraphs or I will be tempted to put it down. Finally, I do not equate the words *boring* and *hard*. Not every text should go down easy. *The Whole Shebang* certainly did not. The work of Timothy Ferris was a hard read about scientific theories on the origins of our universe. I read every word because the author rewarded me on every page, which became an invitation to turn the page.

—•—

Building a Draft

Back in the day, as they say, I believed that writing began when I sat down in front of my Remington portable typewriter to punch out a draft. Now I see how much work must be done *before* the writer can build a draft, a step often stymied by procrastination. Here the writer struggles against bad inertia, the force that keeps her static, and looks for good inertia, the energy that keeps her going. One useful strategy is to *rehearse* before drafting, that is, to accomplish some of the work in your head, especially a good opening or introduction. Reframing procrastination as rehearsal gets the daydreaming writer off the hook and turns a paralyzing force into something productive.

Even when the writer has selected the best material from research, she must decide on an order for the major elements.

The writer searches for the building blocks of the work, as well as an efficient blueprint for the whole. The writer can select a genre, form, or format that already exists—a sonnet, a business letter, a Tweet, a slide show, a graphic novel—or create a new one. Whatever the architecture of the final work, it will be judged by three of its parts: beginning, middle, and end.

If the writer attended to the earlier steps, building a draft should become an elegant and fluent task, but this is not always the case. The writer can still become blocked, not by technical matters but by emotional and cognitive confusion. A destructive perfectionism can leave the writer with the bar set too high. Or perhaps the impostor syndrome kicks in, a lack of confidence that leaves the writer feeling that the flaws in the work—and in the word worker—will be discovered and exposed.

Problems covered in this chapter:

WRITER'S BLOCK

Every writer faces this famous problem at one time or another, but none so dramatically as the character played by Jack Nicholson in *The Shining*. What a shock to see that every page of this homicidal writer's thick manuscript contains the same sentence: "All work and no play makes Jack a dull boy." Solution: Take ax, attack family.

Be assured there are better solutions to writer's block.

What causes writer's block? Counterproductive perfectionism, personal distractions, a lack of preparation—all contribute to that dull aching sensation that we have nothing to say. As you will see, I have gathered time-tested strategies to help you overcome each obstacle and gain momentum.

STALLED ON THE TRACKS

Procrastination is not the same as writer's block. A blocked writer tries to begin a draft but can't find the words to get things moving. Often, this writer has high standards, which can get in the way of a prose that flows. To break through a block, the canny writer learns to ease up and let the fingers do the writing.

If writer's block is the product of a useless perfectionism, then procrastination is what psychologists would call a "cognitive distortion," a way of perceiving the work that undermines the writer. The procrastinator is often overwhelmed or distracted. While the blocked writer may sit frozen at the keyboard, the procrastinator is easily seduced by all things near at hand that feel more pressing or convenient or pleasurable than building a draft. Things like lunch, television, shopping, checking your e-mail, or updating your social-network status for the third time today. Maybe you announce on Twitter: "Story due this week, but I can't get started. I keep putting it off waiting for adrenaline to kick in."

Change the language, change the experience. When procrastination becomes rehearsal, a perceived failure can turn into something useful: mental and physical preparation. "I'm not wasting time," you can tell your editor, teacher, or mother. "I'm rehearsing."

NO PLAN

The ability to organize your materials does not mean that you can also organize a story. Writers use words like *order, structure, plan, blueprint, architecture, arc, sequence,* and *narrative line* to describe the need to put the parts together. When the parts fit, the effect is grand for both reader and writer. We call that effect "coherence."

Just as a house is constructed on an empty lot, so a story fills up empty space. Some of the vessels that hold our writing are prefabricated. In some contexts, these molds are called genres or story types. Some containers are quite big (poetry, for example). And others are smaller and more particular (the fourteen-line rhyming poem called a sonnet).

Journalists and other nonfiction writers sometimes inherit certain story forms (the inverted pyramid, the hourglass, the broken line); just as often, they create their own forms to fulfill a particular story's function. The writer does not have to get all Gothic to build cathedrals of words. On many occasions, the holy trinity of beginning, middle, and end will get the job done.

REFLECT

- Do you work from a plan or an outline? If so, what does it look like?
- At what point in the process would a plan or blueprint be useful to you?
- Do you need a plan for every story or just for the most complicated?
- Can you see the structure of the story before you write it, or do you need to discover it while you are drafting?
- Do you consider yourself a slow or a fast writer, or somewhere in between?

- Does writing on deadline help you through the drafting process or hurt you?
- What obstacles stand in the way of your making progress on a draft?
- When you procrastinate, what do you do instead of writing?

13

—•—

I am totally blocked.

Lower your standards at the beginning of the process.
Raise them later.

This advice, which I now see everywhere, was issued most famously by poet William Stafford, who wrote:

> I believe that the so-called "writing block" is a product of some kind of disproportion between your standards and your performance.... One should lower his standards until there is no felt threshold to go over in writing. It's easy to write. You just shouldn't have standards that inhibit you from writing.

Stafford not only preached that advice, he also practiced it, producing fifty books in his lifetime, an accomplishment that led to the criticism that he was "too prolific," an insult most writers would love to hear: "You know, Mr. Shakespeare, you have written so many bloody plays, first *Hamlet,* then *Othello,* then *King Lear,* then *Macbeth.* We think you'd write better if you wrote less!"

When I did a Google search of the phrase "lower your standards" I raised more than 88 million links, including many to Stafford's advice; but I found many other areas of life in which the advice is offered, most often, it seems, in dating. "Can't find your soul mate? Your ideal partner? Then lower your standards."

The key is to lower your standards *at the beginning of the process.* Get that fantasy of winning prizes or of capturing hearts out of your head. When you hit a writing jackpot, it will feel most satisfying, but it will not help you write your next story.

Try to imagine the story in your head.

Writing begins before your hands start moving. Think of your writing preparation time as something positive, a process of rehearsal rather than a failure to get started. The more of this head work you do before you begin to draft, the easier the hand work will be.

I've been writing my story in my head since I was a child, imagining myself as a character in an adventure novel or an action movie. What would happen if the bad guys came into this restaurant, guns blazing? While everyone else is eating, I notice some suspicious characters at the door. I dial 911 on my cell phone, calmly walk to the front entrance, then, with breathtaking speed, grab a broom and slide it through the door handles to block entry. Seeing that they have been detected, and hearing the sirens in the distance, the bad guys scamper away. This fantasy never happened, of course, nor did the other thousand similar daydreams. But it proves that narrative is so ingrained in our collective consciousness, we can tap into our story imaginations, piecing together bits of real life observed and other stories remembered.

We have covered the many steps you can take before writing a draft, and some of those can go on in your mind, conscious or unconscious. You can imagine how the story will begin or end; or what the five big parts of your story will look like; or what tone, theme, or voice you are striving for. With practice, you will learn how to "write" the story in your head from conception to final draft.

Rehearse the beginning by speaking it to another person.

You can draft a story with your voice before you write it down with your hands. All you need is a friend willing to listen and maybe ask a few questions. Even an attentive dog will do, preferably a Jack Russell terrier.

Not long ago, I woke to news that filled me with outrage. A famous college football coach threatened a young reporter in front of his peers for some imagined transgression. As I was heating up to write, I began to compose an essay in my head, but my reasoning was scrambled. I reached for the phone and called a local sports radio program. When I got on the air, the two hosts gave me a minute to express my opinion: that the coach was a bully, that the reporter was the bigger man, and that the university should stand behind its reporter, not its popular coach. By the time I hung up, the structure of the column was ringing in my ears and flashing before my eyes. In two hours I completed a thousand-word essay that earned me my first spot on ESPN.com—along with a five-hundred-dollar check.

As a bright high school student, Krystal Heinzen, now an attorney, would break through her writer's block by calling into her room a little poodle named CeSar, after a giant pink hotel on St. Pete Beach. "I don't know how he did it," Krystal testified, "but I'd tell CeSar how bad the writing was going and why I couldn't get started, and he'd sit there with sympathetic eyes and cock his little head, and suddenly I would think of how the story might go and where to begin." It was as if the literary pooch projected a writing idea into Krystal's mind. Of course it was not the listening dog but the speaking writer who did the trick.

Don't write the story yet, but write a memo to yourself about the story.

When you write a memo to yourself, you instinctively lower your standards in a productive way. Once your hands get moving on an informal draft, words begin to flow. The parable on this point involves famous New Journalist Tom Wolfe writing a profile of a stock-car driver for *Esquire* magazine. Wolfe, in the words of this problem's title, was totally blocked. In his frustration, he decided to write a memo to *Esquire* editor Clay Felker. The act of writing "Dear Clay" atop a blank page was like opening the floodgates; the prose came pouring out. According to one version, Felker took off the salutation and put the rest into his magazine.

There is a useful name for such an escape strategy. It is called *scaffolding*.

In the construction world, a scaffold is a "temporary platform" erected so that workers can build a permanent structure. There comes a point when the scaffold has served its purpose and is disassembled. All that remains is the skyscraper, college dorm, or cathedral.

So when Tom Wolfe wrote "Dear Clay" atop his narrative, he was saying, in effect: I don't think I have a story yet, so I'm going to frame this as a memo. It took his editor to identify Wolfe's quirk as a strategy, a scaffold that had to be disassembled so that the story could be seen in all its glory. When you can't get your hands moving on the story, turn the story into something else: a memo, a journal entry, a letter, a note to a friend, a grocery list, anything that blows up the logjam.

Write as fast as you can for ten minutes — without stopping.

The godparent of freewriting is a teacher and scholar with the wonderful name of Peter Elbow. In his influential work *Writing Without Teachers,* Elbow argues for an inversion of the usual model that we must *think* of something meaningful and then *find the words* to say it. The desire to get the beginning just right — or premature attempts to self-edit a draft — are "formulas for failure," according to Elbow, "and probably a secret tactic to make yourself give up writing."

Why not use the physical act of writing to discover what it is you want to say? In its usual form, this means sitting down at the keyboard, or with paper and pencil, and committing yourself to, say, ten minutes of uninterrupted scribbling. When I teach this technique, I give writers a deadline of five minutes, so that the writing is not only free, but fast.

Skeptics wonder if such indiscriminate work produces anything but trash. Perhaps, says Elbow, but the trash may be hiding treasure. It then becomes the writer's job to identify the telling detail or the surprising revelation, and, through multiple revisions, to purge the junk and enshrine the jewels.

"It boils down to something very simple," writes Elbow (gosh, how I love that name). "If you do freewriting regularly, much or most of it will be far inferior to what you can produce through care and rewriting. But the *good* bits will be much better than anything else you can produce by any other method." In general, I do not write freely as a way of getting into every story. But there have been times when I've been stuck and have tried it, and it worked.

Tell the critical voice in your head to "shut up!"

I love to sing, but I rarely did it in public until I was well into my thirties. Now I do it all the time and have performed with friends for thousands of people across the globe. I once sang "Wooly Bully" in front of a cheering crowd in Singapore. I've been known to burst into song during a lecture to illustrate a point about reading or writing. I've even performed for two thousand teachers in a Gothic cathedral.

Oh, by the way, I'm not a very good singer. "Every time you sing," said my friend Keith Woods, "you are taking a risk." A risk to look foolish, to flop, to fail, to flunk—and that's just the F's. So before I belt one out, I have to tell that critical voice in my brain to shut up. Psychologists call that voice the "watcher at the gate," the negative force that wards off all creative impulses.

That watcher keeps a sharp eye on writers. Most early

writing is preliminary, which is to say tentative, experimental, good enough for now. Because early prose is unperfected, it can jump up and bite us right in the associative imagination. That is, we may fall into the trap that expresses itself in this internal dialogue:

> *You:* Hmmm. That's not a very good first sentence. If all my sentences are like that one, this will be a terrible story and people will not think well of me.
>
> *Your Internal Critic:* Yes, Big-Shot Writer, that sentence sucks. Bad writers write bad sentences, so you must suck too.
>
> *You:* Oh, my god, if anyone sees this, I'll be exposed as a fraud. I better stop writing now.

You can call that critical voice on stage during revision, but for now, instruct it to return to the green room.

If you are blocked in your usual writing place, try a new place.

Every writer needs about a half-dozen reliable places to work. Here are mine, in order of comfort and productivity:

- Desk at work (where I am writing now)
- Desk at home
- Recliner in a back room at home
- In an airport waiting for a plane
- On a plane
- At my mother-in-law's kitchen table

Necessity can become the mother of invention, as when you are sitting three hours waiting for that late airplane to arrive. In fact, I wrote the complete outline for *Help!* during flights from Tampa to Denmark and back. Stuck in planes for fourteen hours? Write a book.

At my desks at home and at the office I write on a computer. In most other places, I write by hand with my favorite Poynter Institute pen and a spiral notebook. When I am stuck, staring at a blank computer screen, I will often rise to my feet, lower myself into a more comfortable chair, and write for a while by hand. Making the move almost always breaks through the block. Soon I am back at the computer, making real progress.

It may also help you to become a mobile writer. By that I mean a writer who uses the walk around the park or the drive to the beach not as procrastination but as a form of rehearsing the story. Just as some crabby children stop crying and fall asleep as soon as they get into the car, I am one of those blocked writers who relax behind the wheel. Call it driving around the block. Writer's block, that is.

Write on a legal pad.

Even preliminary drafts can have that finished look on a computer screen, which is always dangerous. It may artificially exalt your standards too early in the process. Or, toward revision, it may lull you into thinking that a piece that *looks* good must *be* good.

I have a collection of books that show the handwritten drafts of famous stories, poems, and songs. In *Songs in the Rough*, you will find Willie Denson's first draft of the Shirelles hit "Mama Said," scrawled on a half page torn out of a school notebook. What's survived of the handwritten version of Bobby Pickett's "Monster Mash" is barely legible, a piece of lined paper mottled with ink blots. Doc Pomus wrote "Save the Last Dance for Me" in the margins of a wedding invitation. "Heartbreak Hotel" and "Wake Up Little Susie" appear written on yellow pads. And Robin Gibb wrote "Stayin' Alive" on a British Airways boarding pass.

Write when the spirit hits you, and that may require a set of old-school tools. I know writers who keep tiny notebooks or index cards with them to mark down story ideas, who have pieces of paper on a night table for scribbling—in the dark— visions and revisions that come to them in their dreams. Write preliminary words in the margins of book pages or even on the insides of book dust jackets. Who knows? Maybe those earliest of early drafts, what scholar Vera John-Steiner calls "notebooks of the mind," will be preserved by a loved one and enshrined in a family album, or the Library of Congress.

Yellow paper announces to the critic, internal or external, "Step back. Just getting started."

Get someone to ask you questions about your story.

I told a story at a dinner party about our high school bus driver, a man we knew as Bussie. He was a wild man of the first order, driving us to school at high speeds, over curbs, into potholes and ditches, through empty lots. As a graduation present, Bussie handed out cans of beer, and knocked back a few himself. These acts were probably criminal even then, but we loved him just the same.

"Have you written that?" asked a friend, choking with laughter.

And so I did: "Borne to Be Wild," still one of my most popular essays. My pal's question lit a writing fuse. And I exploded.

When I try to help writers get unstuck, I often rely on these kinds of questions:

- How's it going? How can I help you?
- What are you thinking?
- What's your story about? What's it *really* about?
- What happened? Who did what?
- What or who do you want your readers to remember?
- What most surprised you about this?
- What was the most interesting thing you learned? The most significant?

Notice that all these questions are open-ended, which means that I can't know the answer until the writer informs me. These are not directives in disguise. The writer is still the expert. If you can't find someone to coach you, try asking these questions of yourself.

Forget the beginning for now. Write the ending first.

One of America's best writers, David Finkel, is a bleeder, not a speeder. His drafts evolve slowly, very slowly; yet he meets his deadlines because his deliberateness produces clean work, almost ready for publication. I could not write this way. But his method of one word after another, one sentence after another until it's just right, works for David. If such straight-line writing works for you, keep doing it.

But when you approach a roadblock, don't be afraid to take a detour. Perhaps you can begin drafting somewhere in the middle of the work. Or, and this one works for me, you can imagine where the work might end.

In 1999 I wrote a serial novel, *Ain't Done Yet,* published over thirty days in two dozen newspapers. My mystery thriller with millennial themes was my first serious venture into fiction, and it was guided by an idea for the end: that the climactic battle between good and evil would occur at midnight on December 31, 1999, at the top of a high bridge during a fierce tropical storm. That climax helped form everything that led up to it, including the fact that my protagonist, Max Timlin, would be afraid of heights (the high bridge) and of lightning (the storm). You'll write faster if you know where you're going.

Novelist Katherine Anne Porter put it more strongly in her interview with the *Paris Review.* "If I didn't know the ending of a story, I wouldn't begin. I always write my last lines, my last paragraph, my last page first, and then I go back and work towards it. I know where I'm going. I know what my goal is. And how I get there is God's grace."

14

—•—

I can't stop procrastinating.

Don't call it procrastination, call it rehearsal.

Rehearsal takes many forms and often wears the cloak of use-less eccentricities. As a columnist, Frank Barrows was famous for the elaborate routines that prepared him for deadline work. Others in the newsroom would watch as he approached his desk carrying two large bottles of Tab. He would then don a pair of airport noise-blocking headphones to create the illusion of serene isolation. He'd reach into his desk and pull out a large leather belt and strap himself into his chair. He was now ready to write.

I've never met a person who did not or could not rehearse. Donald Murray would ask writers to remember times when they asked a boss for a raise or asked someone out on a date or proposed marriage. Each of us testified to our own forms of rehearsal. When things are at stake — and time is not a factor — we don't blurt things out. We create a mental checklist of what we want to say.

Rehearsal can take written forms. Murray told the story of a *Boston Globe* reporter working on a tight deadline. "We need it in half an hour," said the editor. "Great," said the reporter, "I've got time for dinner." Murray followed the reporter to the cafeteria, where he watched him munch on a bagel and slurp a cup of coffee. Then the reporter took his pen and began making a short list on the back of a napkin, a brainstormed plan that would prepare him to draft at lightning speed.

Impose a deadline on yourself.

Solve this riddle: When does a deadline become a lifeline?

The answer: When it's self-imposed.

Many writers procrastinate until the deadline roars toward them like a train, the writer standing on the tracks. Pressing a deadline is a devil-may-care form of exhibitionism, a Houdini escape from a straitjacket, just in the nick of time, fueled by adrenaline. The literary daredevil may self-medicate with caffeine or nicotine to stimulate the writing, but adrenaline remains the writer's best friend — and the drug of choice.

Spitting in the eye of a deadline is risky business for any writer. Beyond the dangers of self-medication, the writer can (1) have an anxiety attack, (2) be punished for getting the work in late, (3) leave no time for revision, and (4) leave no time for editors and other collaborators to do their best work. Not one of these comes into play when the writer sets an artificial deadline.

Author Jaipi Sixbear describes on Yahoo's Associated Content website how writers working online can be both productive and punctual:

> Remember to write your assignments two days ahead of their due date whenever possible. You can even trick yourself into meeting deadlines easily. Put an earlier due date on your outline. Chances are, you won't have time to look up the actual date due. Your editor will be impressed with your promptness.

This process can work by the year, the week, or the day. If it is noon and your story is due at six P.M., impose a four P.M. deadline on yourself and use the extra two hours to improve the story.

Make a list of three things you hope to accomplish in that day's writing.

For example: "I will revise chapter one; I will review my files for chapter two; I want to write the first three paragraphs of chapter two, maybe more." Turning your secret motivations into real language, even if expressed in a short list, powers you forward. I am not one of those writers who keep a daily calendar of responsibilities. But more and more I recognize the value of turning vague expectations into purposeful action.

To do this well, you must cultivate a daily writing habit along with the virtue of self-forgiveness. "Failure" to complete daily writing chores can discourage the insecure writer, introducing self-doubt, along with those trolls standing under the bridge, hoping to block completion of your project.

Your list will reflect where you think you are in the process and contain tasks such as these:

- Explore: Read the newspaper carefully today, searching for story ideas.
- Gather: Interview Principal Ledbetter about her new dress code for students.
- Organize: Divide my notes into three file folders.
- Focus: Write a memo to myself about possible opening paragraphs.
- Structure: Try to create a five-part plan on a yellow pad.
- Draft: Don't check my e-mail or Facebook account— and turn off my cell phone!—until I have written for at least an hour.
- Revise: Read my draft to see what important piece of information is missing.

Promise yourself a reward after your first hour of writing.

For most of us, the act of writing a draft is too sedentary. The writer may dread lowering into a chair for fear of not being able to reach the eject button. So get up and do something for yourself after each hour of writing: eat, drink, walk, chat, stretch, listen to music. But limit the length of these breaks. (It's 3:30 P.M. and I'm back from a twenty-minute break, which included a bag of animal crackers and a cup of English tea.)

Here are my favorite rewards:

- I'll turn on the television and check the latest news or sports scores.

- When I have made some real progress, I'll watch something trashy, like *The Jerry Springer Show.*
- Sitting too long hurts my eyes, neck, and lower back, so I get up and stretch. It looks strange in the office, but sometimes I get down on the floor to stretch.
- I love to walk, walk, walk through our beautiful building at Poynter to a balcony where I can see the harbor.
- I'll talk with others in the office who look as though they need a break. I am especially attracted to those who maintain a cheerful affect and a good sense of humor. (Avoid downbeat encounters during your break.)
- I eat and drink (no alcohol during work hours, please) and enjoy sharing a snack with others. My work clock and biological clock have become synchronized. I often write in the morning until I begin to feel hungry, and I can time the conclusion of a day's writing to the beginning of my lunch hour.

Create a reliable, comfortable place to write.

I was an altar boy for five years and count it as a good experience. I learned a little Latin, met many people from the parish, and observed the Catholic Church from the inside. One job was to help the priest set the altar for various liturgies.

I like to use that metaphor — setting the altar — to describe the time I take to create a good writing space for myself. Of course, what is comfortable for one writer may be distracting to another. One might prefer a loft, or a basement, or a blanket on the beach. One might need a cat nearby, or a dog, or a yellow parakeet named Jones.

I don't need my space to be shiny clean, but I need it to be uncluttered. Piles of papers and files must be put someplace—a closet, a drawer, a distant corner—where the sight of them will not remind me of the other work I have to do.

Good ambient lighting is more important to my eyes than ever, as is some natural light through a window. I can see a beautiful garden if I turn left, but I only gaze at it as a reward. My computer sits against a mostly blank wall to block out distractions.

The most important elements in my work space include:

- A bulletin board where I can pin up pages and index cards.
- A rolling file rack that I purchased for thirty dollars. It has room for about a hundred hanging files; the ability to wheel it around is a handy advantage.
- A bookcase to shelve the works that will provide the foundation of knowledge for a new piece of writing.
- A comfortable chair away from my computer for reading and research.

Try to adhere to a daily schedule of writing, the same time each day.

At Providence College I used to write at night, on certain projects not until midnight, sometimes typing until dawn on a Remington Noiseless Portable. My great college teacher Rodney Delasanta advised me: "The owl of Minerva [the goddess of wisdom] flies at night." It's been a long time since I pulled an all-nighter, and my preferred writing time now is in the morning after breakfast.

I don't need lots of time to get my work done. Some days, a

half hour can produce a couple of decent pages. More often, I am drafting for an hour or two, between nine and eleven, on occasion cruising until the lunch hour. Notice that I used the word *draft* and not *write* in that last sentence. When I am in the middle of a project, I am "writing" even when I am not at my desk with my hands on the keyboard.

I am writing when I am reviewing my notes. I am writing when I am cleaning out my files. I am writing when I take a break to think for a while about a key word or phrase. I am writing when I am daydreaming late in the afternoon. I am writing when I am in the gym on the treadmill. I am writing in the shower. Especially in the shower. But I want to draft every morning if I possibly can.

Tell a friend what you plan to write.

By talking it through with a friend, you not only rehearse what you may write, but you give yourself a chance to hear what you already know. You also create for yourself a test audience. This, by the way, is great practice for cultivating teachers and pitching stories to editors. A good editor will milk the writer for details before the first words of the story appear on the page:

"What did you see out there?"

"An ambidextrous pitcher. He throws left-handed to lefty hitters, and right-handed to righties."

"Do they let him keep two gloves out on the mound?"

"He has a specially made mitt that has six fingers and two webbings so he can use it on either hand."

"What happens when he faces a switch-hitter?"

"They've had to institute a new rule. In fact, they plan to name it after him."

As you can see, the answers to the editor's questions suggest the parts of a possible story. This kind of dialogue is a gold mine for both writer and editor. The editor can take a first look at the goods delivered by the writer. The writer can discover what he knows and, beyond that, what he did not know that he knew.

Don't stop the day's writing at the end of a chapter or section. Leave a little something for the next day.

A teacher once told me that Hemingway used this technique to avoid a morning of writer's block, especially when he had more hangover than cliff-hanger. It is a strategy I put to good use in 1996 while drafting the thirty chapters of a series called "Three Little Words." The story chronicled the emotional and physical struggles of a woman whose husband of more than twenty years was dying of AIDS.

I had never worked on something so ambitious and needed a routine of writing and editing. At first, I would come into the office early, determined to write about a thousand words by mid-morning, leaving plenty of time for revision. I discovered it was not a good idea to complete a chapter by the end of my writing day, though, so instead of writing a thousand words, I'd stop at eight hundred. Each morning I would finish yesterday's chapter and dive into the new one. No hesitation. No procrastination. No block.

This works well with a writing project that takes weeks or months to complete, but it is just as good for a day. If you are writing against an evening deadline, take your breaks before you finish a section, perhaps before you finish a sentence, so that you can floor the accelerator as soon as your pit stop is over.

When your hands are unavailable for writing — when driving a car, for example — use your head.

Each day before my lunch break, I stop near the front desk and watch the news headlines on a big video screen in our lobby. "Record rains are flooding houses in southern Rhode Island." "Police fire on a getaway car, hitting a child who was sleeping in the backseat." "Should sin taxes on liquor and tobacco products be extended to sugary soft drinks that contribute to childhood obesity?"

As I climb into my car, I begin to imagine how each of these stories might pan out, as if I were writing them myself. Such concepts can be tested by a set of questions:

- "Rhode Island is called the Ocean State, but they say the rivers are rising and causing the flooding. So do high tides contribute to the problem?"
- "Was the child related to the driver, or just the victim in a stolen car? Did the driver even know the child was in the back?"
- "Soda, even if it's not healthy, is a food. So are there plans to tax all the other unhealthy foods? Will they tax my favorite food, pizza?"

You need not be an expert or an assigning editor to ask such questions. Basic curiosity turns brainstormed questions into story elements: a strong beginning, just the right detail, a revealing scene, a boffo ending, all of which can be envisioned before a word is drafted.

Dictate the story into a recorder.

Dictating a story is a tried and true talent of literary artists, and not just reporters. Some of the greatest works of Western literature were dictated by authors who had lost their sight, giants such as John Milton and James Joyce. Many celebrities, politicians, and athletes who work with ghostwriters speak their ideas, opinions, and recollections into recorders for later editing, collating, and transcription.

With mobile telephones and microrecorders everywhere, it is easier than ever to speak a story before drafting. Improving voice-recognition technologies will mean that we can skip a step, no longer having to transcribe the audio. The sound will be converted immediately to text on a screen. Here's an example of such dictation: "Eleven members of a 1992 girls soccer team were inducted into the Lakewood High School sports hall of fame. (I've got to find out the names of the girls who were not there.) The girls, who won a state championship, are now women in their early thirties, and there were little kids running around everywhere. One woman, who could not come because of a serious illness (not sure what it is), was represented by her eight-year-old son. It was very touching." As you can see, this transcript of a recorded message is not a story yet, but having converted thoughts to language in some form, I can sit down and begin to draft in earnest.

15

—•—

I have trouble working from a plan.

Consider whether your material has a transparent beginning, middle, and ending.

Some writers express a desire to create story structures that are invisible to the reader, "seamless," to use a favorite word. They are on the same team as George Orwell, who argued that good writing is like a window pane. In other words, the writing should never occlude a view of the world.

If you write seamless and coherent prose, bless you. If you are like the rest of us, you may have to show the seams, which can offer benefits to the reader and writer alike. Some research on learning has revealed the importance of formal structures to thinking, understanding, and remembering. When you read or hear the word *face,* a familiar pattern comes to mind, one that includes the symmetry of ears, eyes, and nostrils. The same with *buffet*. The same with *guitar*. The same with *résumé*.

The basic structure for written work is beginning, middle, and end. A single sentence can be constructed in three transparent parts: "Roy Peter Clark, who has lost most of his hair, now agrees that bald men are sexy." Try this simple trick: Take your notes and mark your best items as a B, M, or E. See if that leads to a more coherent beginning, middle, and end.

Time is your best friend in story construction, but ask yourself whether the chronology should be straight or loopy.

For narrative writing, the movement of time is of the essence. Draw a timeline and place key scenes in chronological order. In most cases, your story will flow along a straight chronological line: the princess is about to be married; she is kidnapped by a pirate; she kills the pirate and becomes the new captain of the ship. This happens, then this happens, then that happens.

On other occasions, story time is looped rather than straight. The most common of these loops is called a flashback, a versatile strategy that can be used to fill in the background of a character, as when Harry Potter and Dumbledore use a magical memory device to travel back to the childhood of Tom Riddle to discover the forces that turned him into the Dark Lord, the evil Voldemort.

The flashback can be used not just episodically, but with the whole structure. Authors such as John McPhee describe this manipulation of time graphically by envisioning the lowercase letter *e*. It will be easier to see if I make it bigger: **e**. The flat line represents the beginning of the chronology, but the story then loops back to an earlier time and progresses past the point of the beginning.

Even if you use straight chronology, you still have decisions to make. Where will the line begin? When the sky darkens and a sudden squall hits the gulf? When the harbor pilot can no longer see the bridge and tries to turn the huge freighter to a safe stop? When the bridge is destroyed, sending vehicles into the sea? Or perhaps earlier, when the pilot is enjoying his morning coffee?

Use space and geography to organize the work, moving the reader from place to place.

If time doesn't provide you with the order you need, consider space. Take the reader on a tour of key places damaged by the hurricane, earthquake, or tsunami.

The *Philadelphia Inquirer* once produced a story called "A Day in the Life of AIDS." A team of reporters and editors was assigned to identify key locations in the world where the story of AIDS was playing out. All the reporting had to be done in a single day, with the story appearing in the next day's paper. Quite an achievement. And while a clock ticks through the story, this was not a time story but a place story. The key is not what might have happened at ten A.M. or two P.M. The key was to map a network of places where people were suffering, or where people were working to limit the suffering.

The structure of space becomes a key strategy in the interactive world of multimedia. In a video game you may have to choose a door. For an online story about deforestation, the producer may provide a map of the world where users can click on certain countries to learn the effects there.

Some of the best stories, such as the infancy narratives of Christ, combine both time and space as organizing principles. The Roman emperor conducts a census, so Joseph and Mary travel from their home in Nazareth to the birthplace of Joseph, Bethlehem. At the age of thirty, Jesus begins his public ministry, and gospel narratives do not just track the three years until his death, but also visit the many iconic places in and around Judea where Jesus and his followers travel. Time and space.

Build a story around conflict and complications.

Stories depend on certain reliable movements. Early on, something important or interesting happens, usually a complication in the life of a key character. That character must overcome obstacles in search of a resolution. Think of the beginning of almost every episode of *Law & Order*. Two or three people, sometimes adults, sometimes children, act out moments of their daily lives: throwing garbage in the dumpster, stealing a bike, walking the dog, kissing good night, when, out of the blue, one of the characters stumbles upon a corpse. Curiously, we rarely see those characters again. They have served their purpose. It's now up to the police to solve the case, and the district attorneys to prosecute.

Hamlet's father has been murdered and his mother has married the murderer. (Talk about your complications!)

Romeo and Juliet fall in love, but their families are at war with each other.

King Lear foolishly divides his kingdom among his daughters, only to find himself left out in the storm.

Each of these represents the Shakespearean version of a story problem that finds some resolution, in these cases tragic, by the end of the play.

Under the tutelage of Robert McKee, screenwriters build stories around what is called an "inciting incident," an important problem that kicks off the action. The baby Moses is abandoned in a basket on an Egyptian river. Cinderella has a wicked stepmother and can't go to the ball. Rudolph has a shiny red nose and none of the other reindeer will play with him. Scrooge is complaining about Christmas when the ghost of his dead business partner Marley appears to him. JFK is assassinated during a motorcade in Dallas. On a bright September morning, two planes crash into the World Trade Center towers.

Keep the structure simple, such as problem-solution.

In explanatory or expository work, the structure is built less upon narrative action and more upon pragmatic action. One day a young couple buys a new house. In a few weeks the owners notice that white paint is flaking off one of the wooden posts that hold up the front porch. To assess the damage, the man picks at the paint with his finger and suddenly puts his finger right through the post. He isn't Superman. The wood post has been eaten from within by termites, and the homeowners have a problem to solve.

If I were writing a guide for such homeowners, I would create a list of specific actions that could help with their problem. Such a list might include:

- Call your insurance agent. Find out if the previous owner bears some responsibility for repairs.
- Call a roofer to see if a water leak was attracting the termites from the ground.

- Conduct an online search to see how others have dealt with this problem.
- Get recommendations from friends on reliable and honest local exterminators.

The problem-solution structure does not require the writer to divide the whole story in half, describing first the problem and then the solution. Perhaps a problem can be briefly stated (an asteroid is headed toward earth!) with the rest of the story becoming an inventory of possible solutions.

Collect prefabricated structures: the sonnet, the whodunit, the oral history.

If you struggle with story structure, adopt a theory known as Occam's razor, which professes that the best strategy is often the simplest. Look first for forms that exist in literature and nature and reflect the human condition, patterns such as the pilgrimage or the search. Writers need only adapt these to new purposes.

Don't be afraid of reliable language formulas. There are many ways to freshen these, shaping them to meet your immediate goals. As editor Steve Lovelady once said, "It takes a formula to do a backward triple flip off a high board, but that doesn't make it easy, or less wonderful to behold."

There are thousands of such formulas, most of them associated with a specific discourse community (or language group). Police officers have their reports. Lawyers (and underwear models) have their briefs. Publicity writers have their press releases. Japanese poets have their haiku. Your job as a writer is to master the forms that represent the group you want to enter and serve.

Try writing a parody. This advice comes from poet Donald Hall, who notes wisely that in order to make fun of something, you must master its formal requirements. A practitioner of this form of expression is comic Stephen Colbert, whose late-night TV persona is a parody of conservative commentators from Fox News. From the opening credits, the audience sees eagles flying and American flags waving and the hilarious host's blustery posturing.

During a national presidential convention, Colbert wanted to expose the shallow requirement that a candidate must show he came from humble beginnings, no matter his current wealth or power. The comic then declared his own candidacy, proclaiming that he was descended from "goat turd farmers from France."

Place your topic in the middle of a page and map out the subtopics in spokes, creating a wheel of meaning.

This process of mind mapping is well established, a form of exploration in which clusters of meaning are imagined and connections revealed. Gabriele Rico, in her book *Writing the Natural Way*, professes that such work releases the expressive power of the right side of the human brain. Each spoke of this brainstorming wheel has the potential to focus the story.

Take, for example, the news that a county in a poor state no longer has a single doctor to serve those who live there. In the middle of the map you would write the hub of the story, something like NO DOCTOR. From that central problem you create several spokes of significance, logic, or possible consequences.

Spoke #1: Where is nearest doctor—how do people get there—closest emergency room

Spoke #2: Incentives to get more doctors—nearest medical school—scholarships in exchange for terms of service

And so forth. A rich topic can easily spin off a dozen spokes or more. Some story structures will appear from following a particular spoke, others from where spokes connect in the middle to form the wheel.

On a single piece of paper, write a five-part plan.

Five is a productive number that riffs off the magic number three. Five gives you a beginning, a three-part middle, and an ending. The challenge is not imagining this construct, but matching it to the content of the story. You will need time to sort through the material, to organize it into its parts, and then to stack those parts in a meaningful order.

In law school, students learn to write legal arguments according to a five-part structure known by the acronym CREAC: Conclusion, Rules, Explanation, Application, Restated Conclusion. Robert McKee argues that "a story is a design in five parts": Inciting Incident, Progressive Complications, Crisis, Climax, Resolution.

Finding a structure is not unlike playing a game of solitaire. When you begin, the fifty-two cards in the deck are in random order, the result of thorough shuffling and card cutting. To win the game, you will have the cards organized into four piles: hearts, diamonds, spades, clubs. Each of those piles will be stacked in numerical value, king on top and ace on the bottom.

A five-part plan can begin with a simple list of the major

parts of the story: the popularity of pizza; the memory of my first pizza; how soldiers returning from Italy after WWII made pizza more popular in America; the dominant styles of pizza around the globe; the future of pizza. I listed those elements as they came to me. My next job is to stack them in the most coherent and interesting order.

Research how other authors organize their stories.

Generous writers share their tools. Ask a writer of coherent stories to reveal his best strategies for building a piece of writing. A good example comes from Peter Rinearson, who won a Pulitzer Prize in 1983 for a memorable series of stories on Boeing's creation of the 757 jetliner. I called Peter in Seattle and interviewed him on his research and writing techniques. Here's a snippet of what he said about his process:

> In trying to organize it, I said first, "Do I want to tell this story chronologically?" Then I said, "Do I want to tell this story subject by subject?" And neither of them seemed to be the ideal. I mated the two in a sense. The offspring was this format in which I went both chronologically and by theme, trying to find a subject that happened early on in the process and then trying to deal with another subject that centered around a time frame later in the process.... The turning over of the airplane is the final thing.

Some writers are secretive about their methods. Screw them. Don't buy their books. But do not be afraid to reach out to writers who see themselves as part of a community of word workers and who accept responsibility for supporting the entire guild.

If you find a generous writer, ask these kinds of questions:

- What are your three favorite story forms?
- Do you work from a plan? If so, what does it look like?
- Do you ever find it necessary to revise the structure, move the big parts around?

String a sequence of scenes.

The basic unit of storytelling is the scene. Harvest the most important scenes and imagine a sequence of scenes arranged tentatively in chronological order. Sequencing is the spine of a developing story. Things happen in a story, and because they happen in time, the writer must put something first and then something else second. This does not mean that scenes need to be sequenced in strict chronological order, although that is often the case. Flashing back in time (or projecting forward) is a reliable and well-tested strategy in literature and cinema.

You cannot set your sequence in stone until you know the scenes it will contain, which is why compiling scenes on index cards works so well. It allows the writer to experiment with tentative orders and helps the writer figure out not just the order, but which scenes can be combined with others, or which ones should be set in the foreground and which provide a useful backstory.

Play with the index cards, and I don't mean "play" as a metaphor. The construction of a whole story from the sum of its parts is a kind of puzzle. Solving that puzzle is a creative act of critical thinking, which offers the same kind of satisfaction that comes with winning a race or a chess match.

- - · -

Assessing Your Progress

You might think I'd avoid the word *assess* as an example of educational jargon, associated as it is with high-stakes testing of public school students and efforts to evaluate the performance of teachers. But I like *assess*. Among its six letters, it sports four *s*'s. Even better, it derives from the Latin word that means "to sit next to." When I sit next to a writer to help, I listen to her, receive her story, ask questions, and assess her progress. I try to help her answer the question "How am I doing?"

A good teacher knows how to chart the progress of a student during the course of a writing project. The teacher may even have a checklist:

☑ Summarized each chapter of the book
☑ Handed in an annotated bibliography
☑ Submitted thesis statement for approval

A versatile and effective writer must learn how to assess her own progress with the goal of handing in the best possible version of the story in the time allotted. It may seem like an out-of-body experience — to sit next to yourself — but all good writers do it throughout the process.

It's always best to check in with a helper or supervisor to report on and discuss these developments: Have I done the research I'll need to make the writing work? Have I figured out the most important things I want to convey? Will my work adhere to the agreed-upon length? Have I paid enough attention to the most essential parts, especially the middle and ending? And, most important, will I complete the work before deadline in good enough shape to take best advantage of the editing process?

Most writers I know miss their deadlines, at least on occasion, a product of sloppy habits, dilatory routines, or unforeseen circumstances often outside their control. (Hey, if your dog ate your take-home test, you better hope he passes it!)

Timely work throughout the process sets a pace that helps the writer cross the finish line with arms raised. Have you ever noticed how long-distance runners wear sports watches by which they can gauge their interval times? If they fall too far behind their marks, they cannot achieve their personal bests.

Problems covered in this chapter:

SO SLOW

The slow, slow writer creates unintended collateral damage. If you are too slow, you risk missing a deadline or handing in seriously flawed copy on time. The slow writer slows down all other parts of the process. Teachers, graders, editors, copy editors, designers, photo editors, illustrators, all must work under the gun to accommodate the plodder.

That said, there is no death penalty for writers. Even fabricators and plagiarists have been known to get off scot-free. So the word *deadline* should be recognized for what it is: hyperbole. No one actually dies! Still, the ravages of time can be destructive for all the stakeholders in the writing and reading process, which is why meeting deadline stands near the top of most writing imperatives. On some days it will not be your most important duty, but it is almost always among the top three.

All writers miss deadlines. The fewer you miss, the happier and more productive you will be. Missing deadlines is a symptom of two writing syndromes. There is the perfectionist who cannot bear to give up the story, who wants to make just one more phone call or just one more set of revisions; and there is the writer with sloppy or inefficient work habits. The work does not flow steadily for her, and time and energy can be lost from a lack of organization. If missing deadlines is your problem, your problem is *not* missing deadlines. It can be found earlier in the process.

MIDDLE NEGLECT

Flabby middles and saggy bottoms may be inevitable effects of middle age, especially for writers whose style of life is too sedentary. But stories shape up that way as well: lean, muscular opening, flabby middle, saggy bottom.

Any honest assessment will reveal that writers could improve in the measuring out of their time and energy. Time and energy may be friendly to the writer at the beginning of a project, but as they dissipate, the writer may not be able to keep the pace set at the beginning. Time shrinks even more, the writer accelerates to meet deadline, and the bottom half gets less attention than it deserves.

ENDING ANGST

Have you ever walked out of a movie and thought, "That ending sucked! What were they thinking?" Nothing spoils a story more than a weak or inappropriate ending. Nothing can redeem a flawed story as much as a satisfying payoff. Have you left yourself enough time and energy to create a great ending or, when you are not making progress, will it be your ending that takes the biggest hit?

The skillful writer builds a repertoire of ending strategies, equal to the one she has for beginnings. Taking cues from novels, plays, movies, and music, the writer taps into a tradition of creative conclusions. Songs can build to a crescendo, fade out, or stop short; and there are equivalents to those effects in the craft of storytelling.

The writer faces many problems in establishing an endgame. Time may run out, or space on the page, so that the ending really says, "I stopped writing here." The story may lack focus or a problem may not be clearly defined so that an ending strategy appears forced or contrived.

REFLECT

- Do you think of yourself as slow, fast, or somewhere in between?
- When are you fast? What makes you slow?
- How often do you miss a work deadline, and why?
- How do your time-management skills in writing compare to those in other parts of your life?
- What parts of the process are hardest for you to get through?
- What do you do when you get stuck?
- What are the signs that you are making progress on your story?
- How do you feel about asking others for help when you reach an impasse?

16

—•—

I'm slow and miss my deadlines.

Evaluate how much time you need to carry out the various parts of the process.

Only the perfect writer — and we know none exists — is equally adept at all stages of the process. This paragon would generate wonderful story ideas, be a ferocious gatherer of story elements, keep the most meticulous files, have the critical-thinking skills that lead to a sharp focus and good choices, have the vision to see the best architecture for the story, and be a fast drafter and a methodical reviser.

It does not work that way. Even the so-called five-tool base-ball player (good glove, good arm, speed, hits for average, hits for power) is better at one thing than others.

Try this: Make your own map of the writing process, using the one in this book as a model if necessary. Keep the steps to fewer than seven. Using a 1-to-10 scoring grid, give yourself a grade according to your fluency and efficiency for each step. Using *Help!*'s seven steps, my report card would look something like:

- Getting started: 10
- Getting my act together: 6
- Finding focus: 9
- Looking for language: 8
- Building a draft: 9
- Assessing my progress: 8
- Making it better: 7

You can conclude that I struggle with organizing my materials and finding time and energy for revision. I'll try to gather tools that help me in those areas.

Practice making certain choices earlier than you think you can.

Although we talk about the writing process as if it were straight, like an assembly line, in practice the steps are spiral and can spin back on themselves. For example, it may be possible, even necessary, to imagine a focus of the story before most of the research has begun. Though not scientific by any measure, the focus often resembles a hypothesis to be tested against the evidence.

Let's say I'm reading the paper one May morning and notice that for the first time in several years, as many boys as girls have achieved status as high school valedictorians. Is this evidence that the era of the academic-slacker boy may be ending? With boys and young men doing so poorly in school at every level compared to girls, this might be a timely story. It would be easy enough to get the gender breakdown for all the high schools in the state. I don't quite have a focus yet, but I'm gaining on it.

For this to work, the writer and editor must agree that decisions on the focus are not fixed. The research must still prove or disprove the hypothesis, and even if the original focus begins to blur, a new and better one may emerge.

Revisit an earlier stage of the process.

Donald Murray, one of the founding parents of the writing process movement in the teaching of English, would chart the process as a set of steps, working downhill from left to right. (To encourage writers, I imagine, Murray never drew his process diagram uphill. Writing can be hard enough without turning the scribe into Sisyphus, pushing that rock endlessly up the hillside.) But Murray would qualify his descriptions of the writing process, insisting that it was not linear but "recursive." Borrowed from mathematics, the term means that the solution to a problem can be found earlier in the equation.

Imagine yourself as a writer who is stuck trying to select the best stuff from your research notes, unable to distinguish the good from the bad from the ugly. In simple language, you can solve this problem by retracing your steps. Perhaps the problem is not your inability to select, but your blurry focus. If you think of the focus as a kind of filter, then a poor focus is like having a filter with holes in it. Unless we screen over those holes, the sand and the gold will sift through indiscriminately.

Or perhaps the focus is strong, but the writer has failed to gather enough evidence to support it. That would suggest a need to return to the research or reporting stage. The general problem-solving advice "Let's take a step back here" works for the writer in this situation. In the end, this recursion will save time, not waste it.

Establish a set of earlier artificial deadlines.

I am happy to report that I am making good use of this strategy as I move toward the end of this sentence. I write this on June 9, 2010. It is a solution to problem 16, on the way to twenty-one problems in all. In other words, I've written a draft that covers about 75 percent of a full manuscript. The work has been going quickly, much more quickly than my last book, *The Glamour of Grammar*. For that book I had to renegotiate a deadline with my publisher. My contractual obligation for this book requires me to meet a January 31 deadline. When I agreed to that date, I knew that it would serve as a kind of safety net. In fact, I wanted to turn in a manuscript by the end of 2010, so that the book could be published in September 2011 instead of 2012.

To make that deadline, I established another one for myself: Labor Day, September 6, 2010. To make sure I hit that mark, I've created another one, July 4. At my current rate of productivity, I may not be able to meet that deadline, especially with some travel approaching, but who knows? Just remember this: Any deadline you establish for yourself will be more helpful than one imposed upon you by an editor, publisher, or teacher. (I finished a complete draft on July 2, about six months ahead of schedule.) "Unheard of," said my editor, Tracy Behar.

Don't let yourself off the hook.

We've all seen this scenario in sports: An athlete or a team gets a big lead in an important game and then, to use the cliché, they "take their foot off the gas." Sitting back, playing a prevent defense, chewing up the clock—all such strategies give opponents an opportunity to catch up.

To apply this analogy to writing, the disciplined writer—especially one who has set a series of artificial deadlines—often finds himself way ahead of the real deadline. "Oh," thinks the writer, "I'm way ahead of schedule. I've got time to take that car trip to the Grand Canyon now and still get back in time to finish my book before deadline." I can't tell you how dangerous this attitude is. Small rewards are crucial to making progress, but these should be interludes, not epochs.

True progress in writing comes from habitual behavior. I would predict a greater ability to make deadline with a highly polished work if the writer is the kind who gets up early, has a hearty breakfast and good coffee, and then heads to the keyboard for an hour or two every day. In the splendid multiplication proposed by Donald Murray, a page a day—250 words—equals a book a year.

Don't let yourself off the hook. How much better to exercise one hour every day than seven hours on Saturday. I have next to my desk Murray's favorite saying, one he handed out on laminated cards. It comes from Roman rhetoricians: "Nulla dies sine linea," or, for the Latin-challenged among us: "Never a day without a line."

Send up a flare when you feel you are drowning.

Where can you find a lifeline when approaching deadline? If you were in a lifeboat on a stormy sea and thought rescuers were nearby, you might send up a flare. That's good advice for writers too, especially those working without much oversight. If your story turns in some odd directions, editors need to know. If you are drowning in material and your lifeboat is headed for a whirlpool, send up a flare, alerting those who can help you.

In spite of their reputation as delicate flowers that need nurturing in hothouses, most writers I know, men and women, maintain a pose of machismo/machisma to ward off any sense that they are needy. To ask for help smells of weakness or a lack of independence. Get over it, writers. Writing is a social activity. You need your colleagues to do your best work, and they need you. Asking for help saves time! Yours and your editors'. The alternative is to hand in something deficient. Your draft may be in on time, but it may be in such bad shape that it needs fixing by an editor. Fixing a broken story on deadline takes time and expends emotional and physical capital. A stitch in time does save nine, Mr. Franklin, and sometimes many more.

Begin revising as early as you can.

All time is not created equal. In fact, it's relative. We know from experience, without traveling at the speed of light, that time can drag or it can race. It's a common experience that "time's winged chariot," to use Marvell's marvelous phrase, speeds faster and faster as we get older. So seize the day, writers.

"My newspaper is a participatory democracy," said former

editor Gene Roberts, "until an hour before deadline, and then it's an absolute monarchy." If a writer has, say, ten hours to work on a story, that writer will lose more and more control of the story to editors as the deadline draws closer. That last hour before deadline is a short sixty minutes.

The first three hours of the process are different. Those hours are roomier, to change the metaphor from time to space. (In soccer, the more space you have to work in with the ball, the more time you have to make better decisions.)

Even if you hustle near the end of the process, you are more at risk of missing deadline than if you work steadily throughout the day. All of us writers have to be rabbits on certain days, but the turtle writers are more consistent. Time near deadline is precious and should be reserved for last-minute decisions. Time earlier in the process is more flexible, allowing the writer to be more dutiful in revision.

Pay a visit to those downstream.

One of the wisest and crudest expressions of how most organizations work is "Shit flows downhill." It means, among other things, that people with the lowest status in an institution often work the hardest, get paid the least, and have to clean up problems caused by those suits who work upstream.

Writers, even those of low status, can become puffed up, seeing themselves as the center of some imagined universe. Think of a star in some distant galaxy named Narcissus. Such writers, to change the metaphor from stars to racetracks, wear blinders but, unlike thoroughbreds, often arrive late at the finish line. Because of their delay, every single worker in the production process is thrown off course. Photos cannot be selected. Graphic elements cannot be designed. Stories cannot be copyedited. Pages cannot be produced.

One way to neutralize the poison that builds up in this system is to communicate directly with the stakeholders downstream. This may take the form of an apology or at least an explanation of the causes of delay. Often this courtesy call becomes much more: a conversation about the story that not only helps all members of a creative team, but turns into pointed action. Revision will flow more smoothly if you make that part of the process less mechanical and more collaborative.

Know when to hold 'em and when to fold 'em.

This poker reference may be the most famous line ever sung by Kenny Rogers, from his hit "The Gambler." There is even a casino slot machine game that features words and images from the song. "You've got to know when to walk away...and when to run." This is as true for the writer as it is for the cardsharp.

I have collected over the years many stories about writers who could not "give up" the story. Such a writer often begins drafting late, leaving little or no time for revision. So the writer keeps working and working, past the deadline. The editor encourages the writer to finish; or she may have to insist; or yell; or, back in the day, rip the copy out of the typewriter.

The paranoid version of this writer tries to shepherd the story through the production system so that nothing "bad" can happen to it. He may argue about revisions with the assigning editor or disapprove of a headline written by a copy editor. I know of one case in which a writer followed a story all the way through the pressroom, double-checking the copy when it rolled off the presses.

Quirks come with the writer.

The problem grows when hovering over the process curdles collaborative relationships into adversarial ones. Conversations and debates are best conducted early on, when the key players can help point the writer in the most productive direction.

Celebrate making a deadline.

I've argued here in favor of "habitual" writing. Yes, there can and should be interludes of relaxation and refreshment, but if they run too long they can slow a writer's momentum.

To balance such discipline, the writer and the editing team should look for opportunities to reward themselves for good work completed. If you have a book contract, for example, meeting your deadline with a successful draft will result in your getting paid. The arrival of that check from your agent, at least in my family, is cause for ceremonial celebrations, such as a great feast of Italian food and wine at our favorite neighborhood restaurant, Feola's. On special feast days, I've been known to carry my accordion into Sal and Gina's place and play Neapolitan love songs for the patrons.

Small rewards are the best because you can afford more of them. My golfing buddy Mike Hartigan buys himself a new golf shirt every time he breaks eighty. (If I ever shot a round under eighty, I'm sure there would be drinks for the house at the Old Northeast Tavern.) The reward you offer yourself and your friends should be in proportion to the scope of your shared achievement. Work hard. Party harder.

17

—•—

My middles sag.

*

Honor the good middle.

Teacher and editor Jacqui Banaszynski asks writers: How many of you have been praised for a lead you wrote? A few hands. How about your endings? More hands. How about your middles? No hands. Jacqui confesses that she knows no writer who has been praised like this: "Hey, man, that was a great middle you wrote Thursday."

While beginnings and endings get all the attention, all the glory, our middles remain in hiding.

We need a crusade, fellow writers, to exalt the middle. The middle, after all, is the navel of the story, the center of the target, the rock thrown into the pond. Everything ripples out from there.

Think of your middle as a cozy motel stop halfway to your destination.

A standard metaphor describes a story as a journey with the ending as a destination. Chaucer's pilgrims travel on horseback from London to Canterbury, telling tales along the way. Canterbury, the holy city, was the destination, but in the poet's original conception, the pilgrims were to continue their storytelling contest back to London, the city of man. Chaucer ran out of time. Had he finished his "there and back" version, Canterbury, the end point of the journey, would have become the middle.

In many of his five-act plays, Shakespeare turns the third act into a destination, a dramatic high point from which all important consequences flow. In *Hamlet,* the third act is home for the play within a play that proves the guilt of the usurper king. In *King Lear,* it reveals the fallen monarch at his low point, naked on the moor in a ferocious storm.

If it helps, think of the middle as the top of a hill and the story as a journey from the bottom to the peak then back down to ground level.

Up the ante.

The term "up the ante" comes from the world of gambling and means to raise the betting stakes. In a story, it means to have a character solve a complication only to face a surprising and more difficult challenge.

In *Beowulf,* we have a hero who saves a kingdom by hand-to-hand combat with the monster Grendel, but who then must kill Grendel's wicked mother in the depths of a horrible swamp. As if that were not enough fame and honor, he must go on to save his kingdom from an avenging dragon, at the cost of his own life. Up the ante.

Michael Corleone is a civilian in a Mafia family who gets dragged into mob life when rivals try to murder his father. Things get hotter in *The Godfather*, when the rivals succeed in murdering his brother and then his new Italian bride. Up the ante.

Kurt Vonnegut once wrote that to tell a good story you need to take a sympathetic character and spend about three hundred pages or so doing horrible things to him. Think Ulysses, Job, Jesus, Cinderella, Frodo Baggins. The hero may emerge triumphant, but not without the scars of battle. Over the course of the story, those scars grow more prominent to cover wounds that are deeper.

Consider how this works in the *The King's Speech*, the 2010 film based on the true story of King George VI. As it opens, we find a prince, known as Bertie, who suffers from a serious speech impediment, a stammer that turns his occasional public appearances into nightmares. Things happen, and the stakes for the prince and his country grow larger and larger. His father, the king, dies. His older brother abdicates the throne. Bertie becomes king just as that demonic orator, Adolph Hitler, rises to power. With the help of a friend and tutor, the new king must make a radio speech in which he calls his people to unite in a great war against tyranny. The stakes don't get higher than that.

Begin to notice middles in your reading.

You cannot write good middles until you read good middles, and this is best done in collaboration with others. If you are in a book club, make it a point to discuss the middle of the story.

If you work with other writers in an office, notice when someone places something special in the middle.

A poet once described for me a poem with a secret structure: Line one rhymes with line thirty; line two with twenty-nine; line three with twenty-eight, etc. The middle of the poem, lines fifteen and sixteen, form a perfect rhyming couplet. Something similar happens in George Herbert's poem "Easter Wings," in which the varying lengths of twenty lines create the visual emblem of a pair of wings. To accomplish this, the poet makes the first and last lines of each stanza the longest, while the middle lines are the shortest: "Most poor" and "Most thin." These brief phrases in the middle begin to generate longer lines, reflecting the Easter themes of death and rebirth.

Look at the middles of short pieces of writing as well as nonfiction books and novels. Pay attention to the middles of other creative works, such as movies, operas, and songs. In my unpublished novel *Trash Baby*, a boy finds a baby abandoned next to a dumpster and saves its life. A hunt for the mother ensues—she faces criminal charges—until the young hero has an insight that changes everything, an insight that occurs in the structural middle of the story.

Stop using middles as your dumping ground.

A common complaint from writers is that tin-eared editors force them to include background information for readers unfamiliar with an ongoing story. "You think there's a reader who does not know there's been a catastrophic earthquake in Haiti?" argues the frustrated writer. So the writer tries to minimize damage to his otherwise perfect story by hiding the background information—right in the middle of the story.

All the B-roll stuff, the standard archived video, winds up in the middle. This is followed by all the boring stuff. It goes in the middle. Then some clutter of statistics. It's a kind of cynical trick by the writer, opening the story with a catchy lead and then saying essentially to readers: "Suckers. Here's the rest of the crap in my notebook, right where my editor wants it to be, in the middle."

If you require a reminder that the middle of a story needs to be as well-groomed as the top and bottom, place a little sign next to your computer: "No Dumping Allowed."

Reproportion your middle.

Everyone needs a more shapely middle, a six-pack of muscle instead of a beer keg. Examine the structure of your stories to see what percentage of the whole your middle represents. Don't let your stories become like those guys who have such huge beer bellies it's impossible to notice anything else about them. Wives have been known to refer to this effect as "overhang."

Your lead and ending may each represent 10 percent of the whole, making the middle a shapeless blob of 80 percent. Even if you reduce that proportion to 60 percent, the middle will create a reader's pathway from beginning to end. Think of your story, for example, as consisting of five blocks: an introduction (20 percent), a three-part middle (60 percent), an ending (20 percent). In short, shorten your middles.

Strengthen your core.

Any person with a bad back has heard this advice from a doctor or a physical therapist: "You've got to strengthen your core." With stretching and resistance training, a person works on the muscles in and around the stomach, protecting the back, improving posture, building strength, and increasing flexibility.

Carry that analogy to the writing of a story and it will lead you to revisions near the center of your work. Here is why that is so important: Without a strong core, the story will lack an effective bridge from opening to conclusion. Instead of a strong bridge, a weak middle turns into quicksand, trapping the reader and impeding her progress through the story. You don't move through quicksand. You try to escape.

Save a gold coin for the middle.

My friend and mentor Don Fry famously compared the structure of a successful piece of writing to a series of gold coins left along a forest path. The reader walks along the path and finds a coin, and then another, then another. The reader keeps walking until he is sure there are no more rewards to be found.

Editors, infamously, take those gold coins — those special moments in the text — and move them higher in the story. The result is a schizophrenic structure: a treasure trove in the top half, lard down below.

Examine your stories with this image in mind. Make sure there is a bright gold coin, not just at the top and bottom, but in the middle.

Celebrate the crossing of the equator.

Travelers on cruise ships often celebrate the crossing of the equator, that invisible girdle around the globe.

There are ways in which writers can signal the crossing of the equator of a story:

- By letting a character illustrate that a narrative journey is half completed.
- By the occurrence of an important promised event— such as an arrival.
- By the appearance of a story-changing character.
- By the use of subtitles or chapter headings that signify a crossing over.
- By the use of symbolic geography, a landmark or signifi-cant location that marks an important stopping place along the road of the story.

I remember the day when a construction crew reached a benchmark in the completion of a new wing of the Poynter Institute. When the workers had finished building to the high-est point, they raised an American flag and invited everyone to a barbecue lunch. If only writers could be as sensible as con-struction workers.

Tap into the power of ceremony.

The Godfather begins with a lavish wedding and ends with a christening, punctuated by a series of gangland executions. "Do you renounce Satan?" "I do renounce him." Kapow. Kapow. Kapow.

We live our lives through ceremonies, liturgies of begin-nings, endings, or transitions: baptisms, circumcisions, birth-days, weddings, bar mitzvahs, graduations, retirements, wakes, and funerals. While these events often are destinations near the end of a narrative, they can be used effectively in a central location. Families, as we know, can be seen at their best during such ceremonies—and more often at their worst. Romeo and

Juliet, for example, fall in love at a masked ball and die at the end of the play—but it is their secret marriage and consummation that mark the middle.

Soap operas use ceremonies to gather all the characters in one place—as Shakespeare does in the middle of *Hamlet*. Something dramatic—usually something revealed or someone behaving badly—changes the direction of the story.

18

—•—

It never ends well.

*Think of the story as a journey and the ending as a
destination.*

Imagine your writing as a form of cartography. You are creating a map that leads the reader to an important place. You serve
as a narrative GPS, marking the best route from here to there.
The story structure "there and back" is recognized by folk-
lorists and golfers alike (though the golfers know it as "out"
and "in"—front nine, back nine) as an archetypal narrative
form.

Life is a journey, we are told time and again. And it has a
destination, even if we can rarely know whether our timeline is
short or long. Our species is the only one on earth with knowledge of our mortality, which can be seen as a prize of evolution
or a punishment for our fall from paradise. Either way, endings

mean a lot in life, which is probably why we care about them so much in stories.

Collect good endings from books, music, and movies.

To write good endings you need to read good endings, and they appear in all forms and genres, from greeting cards to symphonies to fairy tales. We learn narrative endings from the nursery. They come to us in our favorite rhymes: "...and when she was bad she was horrid." And in wish-fulfillment fairy tales: "...and they lived happily ever after."

Everything that children experience—from travel, to the school year, to stories in books, to movies and television programs, to video games—leaves them with what literary scholar Frank Kermode calls the "sense of an ending."

Check out these endings:

From a Wanda Coleman poem: "wanda wanda wanda i wonder / why ain't you dead."

From the Garret Keizer essay "Loaded": "Give me some people who are not so evolved that they have forgotten what it is to stand firm under fire or even to squat near the fire in a cave. Give me an accountant who can still throw a rock."

From Joseph Heller's novel *Catch-22:* "'Jump!' Major Danby cried. / Yossarian jumped. Nately's whore was hiding just outside the door. The knife came down, missing him by inches, and he took off."

From Mary Shelley's *Frankenstein:* "He was soon borne away by the waves and lost in darkness and distance."

Keep and share your own list of good endings.

Try writing your ending first.

J. K. Rowling knew how her seven-book Harry Potter series would end before she wrote the first words of book one. You can make better progress toward your destination if you can see where you are headed. Rowling was so certain of her omega point that she leaked to her fans that the last word in the final book would be *scar*. She changed her mind, as authors often do, and ended the series with an epilogue that projected the main characters into the future. Her actions demonstrate how valuable a clear destination is for the writer, even if she eventually winds up a little to the east or a little to the west.

Author Jack Riston offers good advice on his blog:

> A successful trip usually starts with a destination. If you are stymied a bit with your story writing, I'm going to suggest that you consider starting your next book with your "destination"…the ending…the last chapter. There is nothing quite like knowing the final outcome of your story…how the main character has solved their issues, how the plot resolved….
>
> I worked on the final chapter of *Mandate* last night, for this very reason….And now I have the remainder…the other 95 percent of the book to write. It was such a powerful and touching ending…that I only hope I can do justice to the chapters that will lead up to the final moments of the book.

Think about an ending from the very beginning of the process.

Think of this as a brainstorming exercise, a freewriting experiment designed to get you to imagine where your story will end.

You may not write the words of a hypothetical ending, but you will do well to search for an end point during your reporting and research, and to rehearse various versions until you draft a final ending.

My first short story was written for a wonderful eighth-grade teacher, Richard McCann. It was back in 1962, when the brilliant fictional defense attorney Perry Mason was winning case after case against District Attorney Hamilton Burger (Ham Burger!). I loved those courtroom dramas and used them to inspire my own effort, titled "The Unsuccessful Failure." Check out the tension in that title; hooray for little me.

The story was about a young defense attorney who had never yet won a case. The pressure was getting to him, giving him terrible headaches (foreshadowing!). He tries a case with a death sentence on the line. Just before the jury returns the verdict, the lawyer collapses on the defense table and dies on the spot of a cerebral hemorrhage before he can hear the words of the verdict, "Not guilty." I can still remember how I wrote that story, and it was clear to me from the beginning that he would drop dead at a moment of dramatic tension, never hearing the words that would have been music to his ears.

Let the ending echo the beginning.

If your beginning is so important, why not remind the reader of it at the end? This works best when the ending teaches us something new about the beginning. This is sometimes called a ring or circle structure, and you will recognize it from the standard motifs of film and fiction.

The Lord of the Rings is a famous trilogy of fantasy novels by J. R. R. Tolkien, which became award-winning movies. The story is now familiar to millions: Frodo Baggins sets out from the Shire under the guidance of Gandalf the wizard to destroy a ring of power so as to liberate the world from the forces of evil. It's a long, long story, filled with wonderful characters and numerous adventures and rescues. In the end, Frodo and his friends make it back home to the Shire. But his arrival is bittersweet. He has closed the circle, but the ravages of war have changed his tidy little world forever.

Moving from epic fiction to short poetry, we can see how Shakespeare uses this same device in the fourteen lines of Sonnet 29. It begins:

> When, in disgrace with fortune and men's eyes,
> I all alone beweep my outcast state...

The narrator of this poem at first bemoans his bad luck and his low reputation and status, his "outcast state." What follows is a brief inventory of his woes and failures, a condition in which he almost despises himself. But then he thinks upon his lover and the joy he brings into the poet's life, and he is transformed:

> For thy sweet love remember'd such wealth brings
> That then I scorn to change my state with kings.

That couplet repeats the word *state,* which for the Elizabethans would denote one's social estate, from peasant to aristocracy. That key word in the opening is repeated at the end, but with hopeful new associations.

Write an epilogue.

Readers are often curious about what happens to the characters after the narrative ends. An epilogue satisfies this curiosity, leaving the reader informed and fulfilled. As a form, the epilogue can appear as a short story unto itself or as a list of characters and what has happened to them.

A controversial example of the first involves the conclusion of the Harry Potter series, part of which, remember, was written by J. K. Rowling early in the process. The main story ends after a great battle between the forces of good and evil devolves into a one-on-one confrontation between Harry and the Dark Lord, Voldemort. There are a few pieces to pick up, such as who lived and who died, but the duel resolves the basic tension of the story. With so many millions of readers invested in these characters, Rowling felt the need to offer something more, a vision of the future in which Harry marries Ginny, and Hermione marries Ron, and they both have children going off to magic school. This happy ending was meant as a payoff for faithful readers, but its superficiality dissatisfied many.

Then there is the infamous epilogue of the movie *Animal House,* in which stop-action frames of the characters contain comic captions describing what happened to them. So the gross-out king, John Blutarsky, becomes a United States senator; and the make-out king, Eric Stratton, becomes a Beverly Hills gynecologist. The desire to know more about characters after the natural ending of a narrative is not a critique of the story, but a compliment to the writer.

Leave readers with information they can use now.

Certain pieces of writing move the reader to action: attend this meeting, buy this product, donate money, offer online feedback, tell a friend. This strategy is less common as a conclusion to stories than it is at the end of reports. The best kinds of reports point the reader to an opportunity for action. This is especially true with reports that offer a civic benefit, such as disaster preparation or recovery. One report describes the nature of earthquake devastation, with whole buildings destroyed, people living on the streets without power, water, food, or medical attention. Many readers will be persuaded that they should do something to help, and responsible writers often direct people on how and where to give.

Another report reminds readers that a tropical storm is brewing in the Gulf. I learn that my city is in danger, that I should gather supplies for evacuation, that I can take refuge in public shelters. Where is my closest shelter? What should I take with me? What can't I take? Can I take my pets? If not, what can I do with my cat and dog?

Moving readers to action is a commercial necessity often driven by advertising. The end of the ad copy for Orbit gum on the back page of *Rolling Stone* magazine urges readers to "Unwrap the new Orbit packs to reveal something surprising underneath." On another page, we read: "If you're a sailor using G-rated language, you're probably hungry. You're not you when you're hungry. So have a Snickers and be yourself again." Got a problem? Here's a solution: Eat a candy bar.

Project the reader into the future. What is likely to happen just beyond the horizon?

The old hotel has burned to the ground, but no one has been seriously injured. What happens next? A criminal investigation for arson? Plans to build a new hotel on the site? Relocation of guests?

The nonfiction book *Crazy* by Pete Earley is both a personal account of a father trying to find help for his mentally ill son and a devastating critique of our failure to create a world in which mental illness is treated humanely. The final chapters not only remind us of what is wrong with the current system, but suggest what society needs to do to make things right.

"As this book documents," writes Earley, "jails and prisons are simply not safe or humane places for the mentally ill.... Because deinstitutionalization was done without a community safety net, a huge gap in the mental health system was created." What follows is a set of recommendations, especially for a reform of the laws on when and how the mentally ill can be committed into safe places devoted to their care.

What will happen next? What could happen next? What would feel right if it happened next? Such questions can lead the writer and reader to a good ending.

Let a character "speak" the ending.

This strategy can be overused, but do not hesitate to quote someone who knows how to speak an ending. That quotation often comes in the form of a wise and witty "sound bite" or piece of dialogue from one of the stakeholders in the story: "We're left with one candidate for mayor who wants to turn the city into a police state," said Clark to the former mayor, "and another who thinks the world was created 6,000 years ago."

It helps to remember that every piece of dramatic literature ends with one of the characters speaking. "For never was a story of more woe," pronounces the Prince of Verona, "Than this of Juliet and her Romeo." Shakespeare gives the final words of *King Lear* to Edgar: "The oldest hath borne most: we that are young / Shall never see so much, nor live so long."

The same effect occurs when a novel is narrated in the first person, as is the case with Holden Caulfield's memorable words at the end of *The Catcher in the Rye:* "It's funny. Don't ever tell anybody anything. If you do, you start missing everybody."

Some editors advise writers that they can use this technique on two conditions: first, that they do not become dependent upon it; and second, that they cannot think of a better ending than the one spoken by a character. "You're the writer," said one editor to a reporter. "The story should end with your words."

Play off a classic ending: riding into the sunset, freeze-frame, a kiss.

The repertoire of conventional endings is small enough that you can learn them all by paying attention to the conclusions of films, novels, and television dramas. Such endings go in and out of fashion, but most have strong roots in the culture of storytelling.

While tragedies end with the death of the main character, comedies end with the projection of life: marriage and the possibility of children. Tragedy is about death, comedy about life. In the 2006 Broadway musical comedy *The Drowsy Chaperone,* the two main lovers prepare to marry, run into problems, then reconcile to exchange vows along with three other couples who have found a way to hook up within the action of the play.

Emma offers Jane Austen's humorous take on marriage as a happy ending:

> The wedding was very much like other weddings, where the parties have no taste for finery or parade; and Mrs. Elton, from the particulars detailed by her husband, thought it all extremely shabby, and very inferior to her own. "Very little white satin, very few lace veils; a most pitiful business! Selina would stare when she heard of it." But, in spite of these deficiencies, the wishes, the hopes, the confidence, the predictions of the small band of true friends who witnessed the ceremony, were fully answered in the perfect happiness of the union.

Austen offers writers a good lesson here: If you are going to use a conventional ending, look for an opportunity to tweak it to offer a little surprise, in this case the complaints of an insufferable critic.

—•—

Making It Better

Productive and effective writers leave time and reserve energy for revision, a step that includes everything from story reconstruction to proofreading. The writer's task is to create a final draft that works for the reader and satisfies the standards of the writer. Showing a draft to a test audience can help. An editor, teacher, or friend can work with the writer to see the unfulfilled potential in an early draft and inspire the writer to make the work better and better.

Writers talk of at least two distinct styles of revision. One type of writer revises by adding important elements to a draft. The other revises by taking weaker stuff out. The first kind is called, according to author Stanley Elkin, the "Putter-Inner"; the second, you guessed it, the "Taker-Outer." The versatile writer needs both skills: the ability to fill holes in a story, and a knowledge of how to sharpen an ax and hack away at the dead wood.

While you need these editing skills to make your work better, you also need those organizational skills that leave enough time in the process to revise. One particular model of the process may help you manage your time and propel you toward revision. In this model, the writing is described as only three steps: prevision, vision, revision. That tidy trinity suggests that one-third of your time and effort should be devoted to revision. Your message is too important to leave revision as an afterthought.

Problems covered in this chapter:

NEED TO REVISE

You spend days or weeks conducting research for a story or report. The hunting and gathering is exhaustive and exhausting. Before you know it, that dark hooded figure we call deadline emerges from the shadows. Now adrenaline kicks in, and you begin writing like the dickens. Faster and faster, the clock ticks like a metronome. And then...finished. Whew. What a relief. A look at the clock. Just in time.

Hold on there, slugger. There should be no joy in Proseville. You have left no time or energy for revision. Or you don't know what to revise—or when.

It's one of the oldest and most reliable slogans of the craft: Writing is rewriting. Wonderful things happen when you commit yourself to revision: You have time to purge a draft of its mistakes and flaws, add important details that have been left out, and make a final decision about what the work is really about, and therefore how it should end.

WAY TOO LONG

When writers achieve creative flow, it can be unstoppable, or un-stopper-able, like Vesuvius or Krakatoa. The result can be a mess, the kind of thing editor Maxwell Perkins confronted when an author presented him with a manuscript measured by the pound. Thousands of pages needed to become hundreds of pages. Perkins claimed he could reduce a manuscript by 10 percent by cutting needless words, but some work requires not plastic surgery, but amputation of a limb or two.

The writer can work through the process of making painful cuts by asking herself four related questions: What *could* be cut? What *should* be cut? What should *not* be cut? What shape will the story take *after* cuts are made?

In general, too long is better than too short. Too long can become just the right length with the application of editing and revising strategies. Only a writer who practices a fierce discipline can perform these cuts alone. It usually takes the eye of another writer, an editor, or a teacher to help the author understand what is most important, what is most interesting, and what can and should be saved for another day. Something deleted from a main story can be saved for a follow-up or published in a blog post—if the content and writing are worthy, of course.

HATING YOUR CRITICS

Some good advice or criticism may be hard to take because of the way it is delivered. Editors and teachers have been known to savage writers, bleeding over texts in rivulets of red ink. Even when a critique is rendered with the writer's feelings in mind, it can hit a wall of resistance. The writer is oversensitive, or controlling, or a diva, or maybe an oversensitive-controlling-diva jerk.

Without constructive criticism, the writer cannot grow. With it, the writer can improve a particular story and all the work that follows. The writer must learn to accept criticism — even when it seems harsh or uninformed — as a reward rather than a punishment. If writing is about cause and effect, criticism reveals the effect and allows the writer to evaluate the power of the cause.

The writer must remember that the acts of reading and writing are transactional. As Louise Rosenblatt described with such insight, the poet may create the text, but it is the reader who makes it a poem. It is not easy to give up some control of the story, to release it into the atmosphere, watching readers choke on its deficiencies or smile with pleasure.

REFLECT

- What percentage of your time do you reserve for revision?
- When you have the time to revise, what kinds of changes do you make?
- How do you respond when an editor or teacher makes suggestions on how to improve the work?
- Do you have the ability to take criticism of your work and turn it into revising action?
- How could you revise your process so that you would have more time and energy for revision?

- Imagine that you can read over a draft of your work three times. What tasks would you try to accomplish in each of the readings?
- Make a list of questions that would help any writer make better revisions.
- If another writer asked you for help, what would you do?

19

—•—

I don't know what to revise and run out of time.

Revise at every stage of the writing process.

In most descriptions of the writing process, including the ones in this book, revision comes at the end. Because the writing process is cyclical rather than linear, fixing revision in last place may lead to a misconception of what is possible. The writer who thinks about the process as some kind of assembly line is more likely to squeeze in revision near the end.

So perhaps we need to place the word *revise* next to every step: We can revise—literally "see again"—the idea, the research plan, the focus and selection, the story architecture, and, yes, the draft. We can revise during all these steps, and we can even revise the revision.

Revise by triage.

The word *triage* comes from the French word "to sort," and refers to the process doctors use to sort patients in a medical emergency. We hear it most often in times of war and disaster, but it is used metaphorically to describe the many times when limited resources force us to give priority to one person or thing over another.

I tend to sort through things in threes, what I sometimes call the Yes, No, Maybe process of selection. Writers can apply this strategy, at least as a metaphor, to composition. For example, I've seen the writing process divided into two parts: writing and rewriting; and in this book I describe a seven-step model.

Try out a simpler three-part model, one that will help you remember that the process (and the written work) has a beginning, a middle, and an end. Call the beginning "pre-vision," which includes the generation of a story idea and the research to support it. The middle then becomes "vision," from focus to first draft. The last third is what we now call "revision." Pre-vision, vision, revision.

This new math is designed to help you think of revision as one-third of the process, rather than one-seventh. If you clarify your thinking, you'll inevitably leave more time for revision. Your other choice is to treat revision like something critically wounded, not worth your care and attention.

Observe the distinction between conceptual revision and production revision.

A standard problem for writers has been the overediting that comes with special projects, when multiple editors feel a need to leave fingerprints on the text. Here's where things get mucked up: Some editors insist on offering conceptual revisions late in the process, when the attention should be on production revision, polishing and perfecting the draft. The issue can affect any writer in any genre who must work with more than one teacher or editor.

Let's make the adjectives *conceptual* and *production* simpler. Divide the writing process into two parts. Call changes that come during the first half of the process "front-end revision"; changes late in the game become "back-end editing" or "back-end revision."

This model requires revision throughout the process, from story idea right up to publication, and sometimes later (to correct an error, for example). The more you revise and perfect the concept with front-end work, the less straining will be necessary close to deadline.

Try zero drafting.

As the name suggests, the zero draft comes before the first draft. It may not even warrant the name "draft." It may be preliminary enough to be called a preview of a draft. The purpose of the zero draft is to explore what you know and what you still need to learn. Because the zero draft comes early, it may have to be written without access to research you will use in a later draft or a final product. In the final work, you may wind up using a small percentage of the stuff in your zero draft.

This is not a waste of your time. For many writers, zero drafting opens the door to the flow of words and gets you to write a first draft earlier than usual. In the end, this early writing will give you more time for revision.

Seek early feedback.

They say that men who are lost don't like to stop for directions. They (we!) prefer to drive around until they get even more lost ("Even loster," as a daughter once said). Guilty as charged. This attitude can be found in writers as well. Asking for writing help, we imagine, is a sign of weakness. Nothing could be further from the truth. A collaborative writer has to be a confident writer, someone who is unafraid of suggestions or criticisms.

The best time to consult with a teacher, for example, is right before and right after the research has been completed. The teacher coaches the writer on what she may discover during her visit to the museum or aquarium. That same teacher, or perhaps another student, debriefs the writer, hoping to nudge her toward a focus. Early consultation saves time near the end, creating space for revisions.

This is how I wrote my doctoral dissertation on Chaucer. My adviser would be spending a summer in Greece, so I made sure to accelerate my research so I could get the timely advice I needed to make great progress while he was gone.

Look for important questions you have not yet answered for the reader.

Readers love an immediate answer to a question generated in a text. There are times, of course, when delay is necessary, especially when the author of a crime novel, for example, is trying to whet the appetite or build suspense. I cruised through more than five hundred pages of Michael Connelly's courtroom drama *The Lincoln Lawyer* before discovering who really committed the murder and why, a conclusion that was well worth the wait.

Unanswered questions, especially important or obvious ones, frustrate the reader and raise doubts about the authority of the writer. You can check for holes in your work all through the process, but especially during revision. Holes come from writers who know too much and from writers who don't know enough. In the first case, the writer has gained so much knowledge through research and reporting that he no longer remembers the strategic ignorance that he brought to the story. He is now something of an expert and makes the mistake of assuming the reader knows what he knows. Or the writer may not have mastered the subject matter and, rather than display ignorance, hides it by exclusion that creates the hole. Perhaps the writer knows what's missing but lacks the time or energy to fill the hole. Surely no one will notice. Get real. Some reader will spot—or fall into—that gaping chasm of misunderstanding. So take a little break, eat a Milky Way bar, grab that shovel, then get back to work.

Check for leaps of logic.

Writers may be more in tune with time than logic, which makes telling and revising a story easier than, say, building an argument. That said, a good story can be spoiled by sloppy editing, as when a filmmaker shows the protagonists in a car that was supposed to have been driven off a cliff in an earlier scene. These problems in narrative continuity can be distracting, even hilarious, as can anachronisms that show someone using a machine or appliance that has yet to be invented.

There are several ways in which logic gets twisted in the mind and work of the writer, which makes revision even more important:

Personal bias can drive the writer to ignore certain evidence in favor of details that support a predisposition, leading to a failure, for example, to grant any ideological opponent a shred of credit for good work.

Cognitive distortions can lead to false conclusions, such as that failure to achieve a goal is the sign of lack of work or effort.

Personal theories, such as a belief that a neighborhood is getting more and more dangerous when statistics show that it is not, often lead to bad policies, such as putting more money into policing than education. The writer provides knowledge that the public can use to make clear-eyed decisions.

A search for a single cause often leads to arguments and information that cannot stand up to the scrutiny of objective analysis, which is why we so often see popular notions and conventional wisdom and urban myths debunked by authors who have the time and discipline to test their premises through revision.

Examine your diction — your language choices. Is it appropriate for your subject and audience?

One of my favorite humorists is the late Jean Shepherd, best known as the author and narrator of *A Christmas Story,* one of the most popular holiday flicks of all time. If you remember the story of Ralphie and his passionate desire to get a BB gun for Christmas, you will recognize Shepherd's storytelling tone as "mock heroic." In another story, Shepherd describes a childhood sweetheart, Daphne Bigelow:

> Daphne walked in a kind of soft haze of approaching dawn. A suggestion always lingered about her that she wasn't there at all. Rosy gold and blue tints flushed and were gone; soft

winds blew. Somewhere exotic birds called out in their sleep
as Daphne drifted into Biology I, trailing mimosa blossoms
and offering ecstasies not yet plumbed by human experience.

The diction—nostalgic romanticism tinged with self-
deprecation—is free of phrases such as, well, *self-deprecation,*
or the kind of language we might find in pulp fiction, words
such as *flesh, grind, grilled,* and *fingered.*

You are unlikely to use the word *mechanistic* in a love letter
or *fondle* to solve a word problem in math. Look for language in
harmony with your purpose. Reading your work aloud helps.
Oral reading requires you to listen to the voice coming off the
page. Is that voice in tune with your intentions? If not, it may
help to evaluate your language choices. Look for an adjective
that describes your intent: outrageous, empathetic, whimsical,
analytical, inspirational…and then analyze the text to make
sure all the elements support this effect.

Place together all the elements that belong together.

Print out the story and in the margins index each paragraph
according to topic: the mayor, her opponents, how they disagree, what others say, what to expect on election day. Be on the
lookout for instances where elements are spread out when they
could be together.

I have now met at least a half-dozen authors who use color
coding as a method of creating the most coherent text. The
process begins with a form of indexing in which, during revision, the author marks each section of the work according to
subtopic, a quick form of content analysis. The writer then
makes a list of the most important subtopics, such as:

Holocaust deniers (Red)
Holocaust survivors (Blue)
Testimony of eyewitnesses (Green)
Photographic records (Purple)
Rise of anti-Semitism (Gold)

Notice that I have assigned a color to each of the categories of content. Using that method, a writer can then take a marker and mark each sentence, or at least each paragraph, with a color to signify the content. The writer sees, for example, three patches of purple, alerting him to the position of information about the photographic records of Nazi concentration camps. Now the writer can make an enlightened decision on whether to keep the purple scattered throughout the copy or bring those elements together in a single coherent passage.

Check every fact. Make each word justify its existence on the page.

This requires tough writer love. Never let a draft go before you have checked it for accuracy and proofread it for typos, mistakes, and dead wood. If you write for a good magazine, your work will be subject to the close attention of fact-checkers, some of whom have been known to sniff out every assumption, exaggeration, and ambiguous usage on the page, often prosecuting the work and cross-examining the author.

Lacking a professional fact-checker or a dutiful copy editor, you must assume responsibility for the accuracy and reliability of your work, which requires time to proofread and revise. There are a thousand paths to getting something wrong in a story, and even the most scrupulous of writers carries around cautionary tales derived from his mistakes.

During tedious revisions of book-length manuscripts, author Thomas French tests his research and is satisfied only when he is able to put a check mark next to every verifiable bit in the text, from dates to quotations to proper names. You know you are speaking to an ethical professional when she asks you, after an interview, to please spell your name. "My name is John Smith: J-o-h-n S-m-i-t-h. Why wouldn't you be able to spell such a simple name?" "Because not long ago I misspelled the name of J-o-n S-m-y-t-h."

20

—•—

My work is way too long.

Mark passages that could be cut in a space crunch.

This strategy is often referred to as the optional trim (or OT for short), and it helps writers and editors decide on deadline what *could* be cut from a story. Perfected by the wire services on behalf of harried news editors, this strategy requires a writer to mark passages that, though desirable, could be deleted in a crunch. In essence OT sends the message "If you need to cut something, you can cut here." In cases where more than one passage is marked, the writer should number them: "If you have to cut for space, please cut #1 first."

The strategy of the optional trim invites this question: If you think the story can do without that passage under *some* circumstances, are you willing to consider whether the passage should be deleted in *all* cases? In other words, consider using the optional trim as a step toward a permanent trim. In most cases, it is you, the writer, who knows the story best, making you the best person to cut it, if your knife is sharp enough and your will strong enough.

Do not compress sentences or paragraphs before you consider larger cuts.

If you have written a draft that is *way* too long, do not bother cutting individual words or phrases. Leave word chopping until the end of the process, when you are working with a draft that is now only *a bit* long. Premature compression of the language will make the text look and feel dense. You are better off locking onto big chunks that *should* be cut.

I can think of no great American writer more famous than novelist Thomas Wolfe for turning in book drafts of almost implausible length. His first novel, *Look Homeward, Angel,* would have amounted to more than eight hundred book pages if most of his manuscript had gone from type to print. It is now part of literary history that Wolfe benefited from the ministrations of Max Perkins at Scribner's. Perkins began by cutting words from every page, figuring that would reduce the manuscript by thirty thousand words, or about 10 percent. He eventually got to the larger task, which I would have tried first. He would turn six-hundred-word passages into six words, cutting whole sections of the book, especially those not deemed central to the main character and his experience. Why cut words and phrases at the front end when you are not yet sure whether that section will survive the bigger cut?

Select the best parts of your draft and let the weaker elements fall away.

This strategy for cutting requires you to identify the parts of your work that *should not* be cut. It works very much like a tool we discussed on how to identify the best elements in your research: Examine your draft and put one, two, or three stars next to each section of the work. Even a short work will have at least three identifiable parts; a long work can have many more. Imagine, for a moment, that your essay is about thirty paragraphs in length, and that the whole can be divided into, say, ten parts. An editor tells you that you have room for only twenty-four paragraphs, so unless you want to leave the cutting to her (I don't!), you've got to find six paragraphs (or two parts) to cut.

Here's what I'm going to do: I will evaluate each of the ten parts in terms of categories such as importance of evidence to my point, predictable interest to the reader, a piece necessary to see the whole. Strongest sections earn a grade of three stars; the next get two; and the weakest get one star. (I could give a section zero stars, of course, but it supports my psychology of revision that every part of a draft has some potential value, just not perhaps to *this* draft. Perhaps a one-star anecdote would earn three stars in another essay.)

In my hypothetical essay, I give six sections three stars; two sections two; two sections one. I realize that if I cut out those two weakest sections, I can meet my deadline and my prescribed line length. Just to be sure, I reread those two sections. Perhaps I'll harvest a word, a phrase, a fact. If not, snip, snip, and I have revised the story to a length the editor can now use.

Tell your obese draft to shape up.

I don't pay too much attention to TV weight-loss shows such as *The Biggest Loser,* although I find it fascinating to see the before and after photos, especially the ones where the newly thin contestant holds out the waistband of her old tentlike jeans. The person in the "before" image looks like a blob. The loss of a hundred pounds or more reveals a once-invisible shape, a frame in which you can now recognize the parts.

Drafts of stories can suffer from obesity. They will seem shapeless until you cut the fat.

My best example concerns the drafting and revision of *The Glamour of Grammar.* Unlike my other books, *Glamour* was commissioned, which is another way of saying that it was someone else's idea, in this case an editor's. "Do you think Roy would like to write a book on grammar?" she asked my agent. Easier said than done. To complete the task, I had to relearn many technical concepts about language, which took more time than I had planned. I worked with my editor on the range of the book, what it would include, what it would leave out. I even had to define and redefine what I meant by the word *grammar,* realizing that my definition was more inclusive than my editor's.

As a result of all this, I missed my deadline, but I was fortunate enough to get a four-month extension. Unburdened of the deadline but retaining a sense of urgency, I drafted a 130,000-word manuscript in six weeks. "Take a look at your contract," said my agent. It called for a 65,000-word manuscript, half the length of my magnum opus.

The big manuscript contained 100 short chapters. My editor did not bother with words or phrases, but began to mark certain chapters as "possible cuts." In other words, she was turning chapters into tree limbs that could be pruned to make the tree healthier in the long run. It was hard to get from 100 chapters to 75, down to 60, down to 55, down to 50, but the result was a leaner and more muscular book.

Discuss the scope of your story early in the process with a teacher or an editor.

William Blundell, author of *The Art and Craft of Feature Writing*, has introduced many useful terms and concepts into the practice of the writer's craft. For me, one of the most useful was the simple word *scope*. That is one great word. It's the name of something you look through, usually requiring a prefix: telescope, micro-scope, peri-scope. My favorite line in any submarine movie is "Up scope!" The Italian word *scopo* means "aim" or "purpose"; the Greek cognate means "target." Scope it out.

The scope of a story, according to Blundell, is not what the story is about, such as the unintended negative consequences of Native American tribes relying on revenues from casino gambling. The writer has to scope out the material until he sees the most significant slice or vector of the topic that will make it manageable for both reader and writer.

It's hard for me to do this on my own, so I need good questions from an editor, teacher, or friend:

- Who are the main stakeholders?
- How much will reform cost, and who will pay for it?
- What do they plan to do next to solve this problem?
- What would happen if revenues were significantly reduced?

Answers to such productive questions lead the writer to a great insight on what the story is about, some options for additional research and reporting, and a much tighter vision of the best length. Such steps will make additional revisions unnecessary.

Check to see if you have chosen the best possible form or genre for your story.

In most cases, the writer will develop a sense of a story's form early in the process, much earlier than during revision. That said, you must be ready to revise your work at any stage of the game, from the identification of an idea right up until it goes to press. A poet may discover after working on a poem for some time that it should not be written in free verse. There are enough rhymes to turn it into a sonnet. Of course, the earlier you make structural decisions, the more you protect yourself from having to tear down the walls of your new house right to the foundation.

I remember the day a group of sportswriters discussed a recent event in the NCAA college basketball tournament. A player who had made more than 90 percent of his free throws missed a crucial one at the end of a game, sinking the hopes of his team. "If you were writing about big misses in college basketball, how would you go about doing it?"

A wonderful writer named Thomas Boswell, who at the time wrote long features called "take-outs," imagined what amounted to a magazine article, looking back on the history of the foul shot and leading to the topic of classic missed shots and their consequences. His friend John Schulian, a prizewinning columnist, took a different turn: "I am looking for one player."

I'm looking for someone who missed a key shot thirty years ago and it's still nagging at him—or maybe he thinks it was the best thing that could have happened to him." Turned loose, Boswell might create a three-thousand-word story, Schulian a thousand words or fewer. Each of them imagined the story through the lens of a particular story form, one that produces work that may take twenty or thirty minutes to read, another that can be polished off by the reader in less than ten minutes.

Such clarity about form facilitates revision from the earliest point in the process. Even so, Schulian may recognize along the way that he has enough interesting material to revise the structure and length of the piece from a newspaper column to a feature story in *Sports Illustrated.*

Negotiate a length and then stick to it.

This is easier said than done—at least for me. Yesterday I turned in a foreword for a book on the history of realism in America. I would be paid $200 for a piece between 500 and 2,000 words. I handed in 2,300. That seems standard for me: delivering 15 percent more than required. I cannot remember a single instance where I turned in 15 percent less.

The problem isn't *writing* a long draft. The trouble comes with *turning in* that draft without an effort to cut it down to size.

What interests me here is how different the professional model is from the academic. I don't believe I ever handed in a term paper, say, that was longer than what was required. I'm not sure that "having more to say" with age and experience is necessarily a good thing.

Length may come as part of any assignment: Write 500

words...or ten pages...or 65,000 words. If not, a target length will help you, and it should be established in consultation with an editor or teacher. This target length is no straitjacket; in fact, it provides comfort, like Mr. Rogers's sweater.

Perhaps it will help to think about length as the distance of the race. A race would not be much fun if the object were to "just run a few miles" or "just run until you get a cramp." It's always better to have a confirmed distance so you can choose a race that fits your stamina, and so you can pace yourself to cover the assigned distance in the best time.

Cut any elements that do not advance the focus of the story.

We've spent a lot of time already on how to focus your writing. In the context of the size of the work, it may help you to remember that story length and focus depend on each other. As quirky writers, we can grow fond of a scene or an anecdote, even when that part does not fit neatly in the whole. But cut we must if that part does not support the main theme.

I would be lying if I told you that I followed my own advice. I confess, instead, that I'm often trying to sneak into my story words or phrases or allusions that are often self-referential, inside jokes with a small group of special readers or friends. For example, any time I can get the phrase "three little words" into a story, I do it, a reference to the title of an embarrassingly long series (twenty-nine parts!) I wrote for the *St. Pete Times* in 1996. See, I did it again.

I've heard about a group of writers who belonged to something called the "Unseen Hand Society." The goal of the club was to sneak the phrase "It was as if an unseen hand..." past the copy desk: "It was as if an unseen hand had erased the phrase from her letter."

Such games are not at the center of this strategy. I'm thinking instead of the infamous porter's scene from *Macbeth*. In the middle of that brutal play, just after the murder of the king by the Macbeths, the porter hears loud knocking at the gate and climbs from his bed hungover, a perfect opportunity to offer the audience his bawdy wisdom on the ill effects of drinking on love performance. Even though it's my favorite scene in the Scottish play, it reminds me of the anecdotes I could not bring myself to delete from a story because they were just so funny or interesting, even when they were only marginal to my message. I hope you have more discipline on these matters than I have shown.

Practice cutting 10 percent, even 20 percent, of any draft you think is "finished."

My former Poynter colleague Chip Scanlan introduced me to the idea of the Ten Percent Club, which assumes you have at least that much flab in any story you think may be ready for publication. Through diet and exercise, it might be possible to reduce my body weight by 10 percent, from 170 pounds to 153. But what if I am fit at 170? I certainly don't want to become anorexic just to achieve some arbitrary goal. That's the problem with a predetermined percentage. It's the *idea* of the 10 percent that makes sense, and it can develop some needed discipline.

Many kinds of cuts will get me where I want to be; my habit is to go after something big. In most cases, I can achieve my 10 percent cut by suctioning out that one section of fatty tissue in the form of a paragraph I've used to explain what is already clear or to provide background when none is needed.

Don't stop after you've made the big cut. On page 10 of his book *On Writing Well*, William Zinsser demonstrates the value of going on a search-and-destroy mission for every bit of clutter, every useless word on a page. From a manuscript page of about 360 words, Zinsser manages to cut about 60 words — more than 16 percent of the whole. He cuts adjectives, adverbs, qualifiers, prepositional phrases. He replaces flabby phrases with tight ones, long phrases with short ones. But remember this: Zinsser is an experienced and highly disciplined editor, capable of making fine distinctions among words and finding in revision the one word that can replace five. All these numbers are arbitrary. A rigorous mind will get you through the tough choices.

Begin the story as close to the end of the narrative line as possible.

Don't start with the plans for the invasion, but with a soldier landing on the shore. Don't begin with the court order, but with the child stepping off the bus. Don't begin with the death of the baseball player's mom six years ago, but with the ninth inning of his perfect game on Mother's Day.

Hamlet begins not with the murder of the king, the prince's father, but with the apparition of his ghost. Although the Synoptic Gospels (Matthew, Mark, and Luke) begin with the infancy narratives, the Gospel of John opens with the ministry of John the Baptist. Jesus lived on earth for thirty-three years, yet John the writer begins his story pretty close to the end, at age thirty.

I learned this strategy from working with children. Take a standard and somewhat tired assignment, "What I Did on My Summer Vacation." I can't tell you how many stories I've read that begin weeks, months, before the actual vacation: the arguments about where the family will go, the preparations, the throwing up in the back of the Escalade. Then, finally, to the amusement park, where the family gets stuck on a stalled roller coaster, upside down, and has to be rescued by the fire department. The writer can always flash back to events in the past. I want that story to begin with the family waiting in line for a ride that will wind up giving them the thrill of a lifetime, or even with them stuck upside down on the roller coaster waiting for help.

21

—•—

I resent criticism and editing.

Reflect on how you handle criticism in other areas of your life.

A Polish author once testified that he resented editing because it resembled Communist authoritarianism. Such a sentiment is harsh but understandable. Each of us brings our personal history to the table of writing, revision, editing, and criticism. Without getting all Freudian, we can easily imagine that harsh parents or tyrants in the classroom can create forms of aversive conditioning that stick with the would-be writer.

There can be no doubt that good editors help writers make the story better. We return to Max Perkins as a model, an editor who worked with the likes of Fitzgerald, Hemingway, and Faulkner. His authors testified that Perkins had two things going for him: an ability to see the unrealized potential in a story, and the human skills required to bring the writer along with him.

Reward the kind of criticism you need.

To break out of a negative Skinner box, the writer must learn to praise the kinds of editing and feedback that she wants. Most effusive in her praise of editors is Lane DeGregory, whose editor, Mike Wilson, helped her win a Pulitzer Prize for feature writing. Lane is an insatiably curious writer and a dogged reporter who admits to a tendency to being blinded by the good. Mike encouraged her to find the "bruise on the apple," the shadowy parts of characters that reveal the moral complexities of human life.

Imagine a conversation with a supportive editor. It requires no ass kissing or kicking, only honest appraisals of good work accomplished: "You were right about that ending. I'm glad you encouraged me to make one more phone call. It worked." Or "You know so much about this town, I find it valuable when you remind me of the history behind some of these concerns."

Pick your battles.

It won't help you to be one of those writers who argue over every comma and semicolon. There are such writers, and when they appear in the office, editors cringe and avoid eye contact. Learn to distinguish between changes to your copy you can live with — and those you can't.

It is my habit, as my editors will testify, to go along with 90 percent of an editor's recommendations. That does not make me editor-whipped. It arms me for battle to defend the 10 percent I think is most important.

There are lots of hills on the battlefield of writer and editor. You must learn to plant your flag on the most important territory. "That would change the focus of the story," I can say with my serious face, and my editor knows I mean it. Or, as I said recently to an editor's suggestion, "No, I *won't* say that— because I don't *believe* that."

Be willing to share control of the story.

I love to play tug-of-war with Riley, my son-in-law's golden retriever. He weighs about eighty pounds and enjoys a tussle over his stuffed purple octopus. He wants to win, of course, but knows the game is no fun for him unless he gives me a chance to tug back. It may appear from a distance that we are two alpha dogs fighting for control, but actually we are "sharing control."

Take out the *tug* and the *war* and you have in my game with Riley a useful analogy for the writer-editor relationship. It is a give-and-take, a deal, a transaction, a dialogue, a debate, a conversation, an argument, a consultation, maybe even a seminar in which each party learns from the other. Sharing control turns a potential adversary into an ally, someone who can shepherd your work past the wolf packs that threaten to devour it.

Encourage editors to bounce problems back to you.

The worst feeling for a writer is when he opens the paper, magazine, website, book, and discovers that something has been changed by an unknown editor late at night without consultation. Even worse, that editor has introduced an error into the story, changing, as once happened to me, the name Mark to Mary. That writer has truly lost control of the work.

To avoid such disasters, invite the editor or teacher to "bounce back" parts of the story that could be improved. "Bounce back" makes the editor sound like a brick wall, but it's really a compliment to the writer. As feature writer Cynthia Gorney once said about Shelby Coffey, her editor at the *Washington Post*, "Usually I know that a story is flawed. I just send it in anyway, because I'm confident that they're going to help me figure out what's wrong with it. A great editor will make you feel like a real trouper, a truly talented person for being able to fix a story, for being able to send something in that's flawed and then make it better."

Establish personal relationships with anyone who influences your work.

If you are a book author, you may never meet in person the editor who works for the publisher. If you are a newspaper writer, you may not know the names of the copy editors who work the late shift. The more anonymous you are to editors, the easier it will be for them to change your work without consultation.

If you have the emotional intelligence of an old tennis racket, go ahead and hide in your locker. If you want to get the best out of those assigned to help you, learn their names and faces. Ask what you can do to make their work easier. Bake or buy them some cookies.

A good running back in football shares praise and credit with the anonymous players on the offensive line. When someone offers you praise, deflect the parts that belong to your helpers. Give them the recognition they deserve.

Avoid guerrilla warfare tactics.

If my advice seems too touchy-feely for a rough-and-tumble writer, consider the alternatives, which I count as two: Play the victim and grumble behind the backs of editors or resort to guerrilla warfare tactics.

My collection of passive-aggressive sneak attacks includes these:

- Never make eye contact with an editor.
- Pick up a phone when the editor approaches.
- Always have a story you are "working on" to avoid assignments.
- Wait for the mean editor to take lunch and then hand your work in to the nice lady.
- Stay out of sight, out of mind.
- Hand in the story as late as possible so no one has time to muck it up.

These may work some of the time, but they also can create so much uncertainty and drama that they suck the joy out of the craft.

Argue about purpose, not preference.

You will never win an argument with an editor or teacher who is dogmatic in his approach to the craft: "I hate stories that begin with anecdotes." Or "Readers never read footnotes." Those are not rules, they are preferences.

Rather than challenge those, turn attention to your purpose:

why you introduced a new character late in the story or why you hooked the ending back to the beginning. Mistakes are by definition accidental. You are not an accidental writer who made a mistake, you are a purposeful and resourceful writer with a strategy designed to create a specific effect. So be specific: "I know a funny story about colon cancer may offend some readers, but people won't get colonoscopies because of their inhibitions. I want to use humor to help them pay attention to lifesaving measures."

Prepare yourself for tough conversations.

In a bad economy, you may be reluctant to anger supervisors who control your fate, but even a little courage can go a long way. Editors have bad habits. So do teachers. Why wouldn't they? Writers know this, which is why we gossip about them behind their backs. Everyone knows Mabel is a disorganized wreck of an editor; everyone, that is, except Mabel, who might be able to change for the better.

Diplomacy softens the blows of a tough conversation: "Mabel, you want me to get my stories in by three o'clock so you have time to edit them—and I get that. But then the story just sits there with no one working on it. I could use that time to improve it. What if we changed the time to 4:30? That ninety minutes would mean a lot to me."

Such conversations will work only if you are willing to take responsibility for your own shortcomings. An admission at the front end helps lower the defenses of your supervisor: "I realize I've been too slow on this project, but I'm ready to do something about it." "That closing anecdote didn't work at all—which is why I need you to be my safety net."

Become a productive critic of other writers' work.

- Ask *how* you can help the writer.
- Ask *when* you can help the writer.
- First tell the writer what works for you in the story.
- Ask the writer for her opinion on the status of the story.
- Get to what needs work, the story's unrealized potential.
- Don't disguise statements as questions.
- Narrate a "movie" of your reading.
- Assess how you are doing as a critic: "Am I making sense?" "Do you find this helpful?"
- Help the writer find other helpers.
- Ask questions about the writer's process.

—•—

We have reached a happy destination: the end of the seven-step process. We are not done yet. We are left with one overarching problem to solve, one that afflicts every writer at one time or another. Framed as a question, it presents itself as a whisper in the ear of the uncertain scribe: "What makes you think you're a writer?" When haunted by this question, "who you gonna call?" *Help! For Writers,* of course.

— • —

Keeping the Faith

.

I have saved the toughest problem for last: the nagging feeling that you lack what it takes to be a writer. This self-doubt eats at the most accomplished writers. Winners of Pulitzer Prizes have been known to acquire paralyzing writer's block immediately upon receiving their award. "The hardest story to write," said one such anointed writer, "is the next one." The writer fears being exposed as a fraud, the prize ripped from her hands.

American culture is not, in general, supportive of writers. As author and editor Jack Hart has noted time and again, we teach writing not as a social literacy but as an individual skill. While we expect all citizens to be able to read, we limit membership into the writing club. A few of us get tapped on the shoulder and told, "You know, you can become a writer." Better to say to a whole class, "You write, and it's the writing that makes you a writer."

Every writer in every newsroom, classroom, or company office has a personal history of approval or rejection when it comes to writing. Even for professionals, that history often includes negative consequences. Maybe someone laughed, inappropriately, at our essay about mental illness. Or a teacher held the story up and ridiculed it in front of the other students. Or an editor took a good story, chopped off the bottom half, and slapped it into print. These experiences create something called "aversive conditioning," the expectation that something bad will happen if we commit ourselves to writing.

Writing, in the end, is a social activity. Even when we isolate ourselves in our writing dens, we have the interests of the readers in mind, and the voice of the editor chirping in our ears. Confidence comes with the mastery of the craft, with the ability to solve problems like those described in *Help! For Writers*.

I hope that *Help!* has persuaded you that you do not need anyone to tap you on the shoulder with a sword and declare that you're a writer. OK, Dear Reader, if you really feel that writers sit around a table in Camelot, please kneel. "I dub thee Sir or Lady Write-a-lot." Now rise and get thee to work.

When your courage and confidence let you down, you can always benefit from an encouraging word. You don't need a writing shrink or cheerleader ("Give me a W...."); you have the ability to lift your own spirits, to weave your own lifeline. If you can't find the words, you can borrow these:

The act of writing is what makes me a writer.

Writing does not belong to a small tribe of professionals. Anyone who tries to grow in the craft earns the right to be called a writer.

Writing will help me learn what it is I want to say.

Writing is not only a form of expression or communication. It is also a form of discovery, a way of learning what you know and what you need to know.

I will try to write a little something every day, and will forgive myself for those days I don't write.

Think of writing as a habit — like exercise. You don't have to do it every day to feel the benefits, but you must practice to grow in the craft.

Even when my hands are not on the keyboard, I can be writing in my mind and in my heart.

Develop all your faculties as a writer: an eye for detail, a curious nose for sniffing out stories, a sympathetic heart, hands for building drafts, feet for tracking down a good story.

To become the writer I want to be, I have to read, write, and talk with others about reading and writing.

These three behaviors are what mark a literate person in any society. Read, write, and talk about reading and writing, and practice these every day.

I am a good and creative person who loves the written word.

Not only does the English language live in you, but you can strive to live inside the English language.

To be respected, I must respect others who try to express themselves in writing.

Not all good writers are generous, but generous writers thrive within a community of writers. Become an active member of our community of writers.

If I need and want help, I must be ready to help other writers.

Writing is a social activity best practiced in collaboration with others. When you work with other writers, you will better understand the craft.

Writing will help make me a better student, worker, parent, and friend.

It has been said that the writer grows a third eye: Work to see the world as a storehouse of story ideas, intensifying your experiences with all others in your life.

The act of writing will make me more alive, alert to the world around me, empathetic to the people I encounter.

A story has the power to transport the reader—and the writer—to another place, another time. Through stories you will meet characters who teach you what it means to be fully and completely and oh so imperfectly human.

25 Favorite Writing Books

—•—

Since publication of *Writing Tools* in 2006 and *The Glamour of Grammar* in 2010, I have been asked many times to identify the books that have most influenced me as a writer, reader, and teacher. The list below is by no means exhaustive. I have taken the unusual step of listing books not in chronological or alphabetical order, but in the order of their formative power on this author. You can share your favorites with me — or offer comments on or corrections for *Help!* — at rclark@poynter.org.

1. *Oxford English Dictionary.* The mother of all dictionaries. Based on historical principles and with millions of examples, the *OED* may be the greatest collaborative work printed in any language.

2. *The American Heritage Dictionary.* I love the pictures, the word histories, the lists of synonyms, and especially advice from the Usage Panel. I have copies scattered about and am

thinking of putting a ragged copy in the trunk of my car, near the jumper cables.

3. *Writing to Deadline,* by Donald M. Murray. Perhaps the most influential writing teacher in American history, Murray was friend and mentor. This book is his most accessible and inspirational, a treasure for anyone who hopes to grow in the craft of nonfiction.

4. *A Collection of Essays,* by George Orwell. Old George seems more relevant than ever. I rely on him for his versatility, his vision, and his clear sense of mission and purpose as an author, expressed in such works as "Why I Write."

5. The King James Bible. I wish I had a sip of whatever the English writers were drinking back in the days of Queen Elizabeth and King James. That culture produced some of the world's great literature, and a translation of the Bible that, for its rhythms and harmonies, towers above the rest.

6. *Language in Thought and Action,* by S. I. Hayakawa. Written in the late 1930s as a text for college students, it remains influential. Most important is Hayakawa's popularization of the Ladder of Abstraction, a lesson with millions of practical language applications.

7. *The Elements of Style,* by William Strunk Jr. and E. B. White. This is the beacon for anyone who aspires to pen a good writing book, a thin volume that has survived more than half a century and sold more than ten million copies.

8. *On Writing Well,* by William Zinsser. I apply one powerful lesson from this book every day I sit down to write: Cut the clutter. Zinsser uses his own writing to demonstrate how easily clutter accumulates and what you need to do to clear it out.

9. *Bird by Bird,* by Anne Lamott. Practicing the writing craft is not enough. We need to live a life of language. Lamott

offers practical advice — but always with a sense of how important reading and writing are in one author's life.

10. *Becoming a Writer,* by Dorothea Brande. One of a number of influential writing books penned by women in the 1930s, this one provides lessons on creativity, coffee, and how to muzzle your inner critic.

11. *Writer's Chapbook,* edited by George Plimpton. One of America's most versatile men of letters, Plimpton curates author interviews published in the *Paris Review.* How comforting to discover that the preeminent writers of the twentieth century suffered many of the challenges and insecurities of the rest of us.

12. *Authors at Work.* This special edition published by the Grolier Club in 1957 contains facsimiles of manuscripts from a museum exhibit. You can trace the handwritten changes in work from the likes of Jane Austen, Percy Shelley, Charles Dickens, and Dylan Thomas.

13. *Brave New World Revisited,* by Aldous Huxley. Among the dystopians of the last century, Huxley proves to be the most prescient. This book collects newspaper essays he wrote twenty-five years after the publication of his most famous novel, *Brave New World.* Every page brings a revelation, especially the chapters on language, politics, and propaganda.

14. *Break, Blow, Burn,* by Camille Paglia. A brilliant re-introduction to forty three of the world's best poems, with stunning insights from one of America's most interesting and controversial critics. Poets chosen for discussion range from Shakespeare to Joni Mitchell.

15. *Editor to Author,* by Maxwell E. Perkins. This collection of letters from famed editor Max Perkins reveals his unique combination of literary insight and emotional intelligence. To

read his letter of appreciation to Scott Fitzgerald after reading the final version of *The Great Gatsby* is to eavesdrop on genius.

16. *Hamlet,* by William Shakespeare. According to critic Harold Bloom, the closest we get to Shakespeare's artistic personality is Act III, Scene ii, in which Hamlet directs the visiting players on how to perform the play within the play. It is a lesson on theatrical realism unmatched by any critic.

17. *Modern English Usage,* by H. W. Fowler. This is the enduring masterwork of one of England's most entertaining and influential language experts. First published in 1927, it was watered down by subsequent editors. I consult this dictionary of usage to untangle my syntax but also to enjoy Fowler's tangy prose.

18. *The New Journalism,* edited by Tom Wolfe. I don't remember reading the stories in this anthology. But I've read, over and over, Wolfe's spirited manifesto on how and why writers of nonfiction should borrow the techniques of novelists, from setting scenes, to reporting details of character, to capturing dialogue.

19. *Story,* by Robert McKee. This is new on my shelf, but I have already been influenced by the notion of how an "inciting incident" fuels a story. McKee is a veteran screenwriter, story doctor, and teacher whose appreciation of great stories will add tools to your workbench.

20. *Literature as Exploration,* by Louise M. Rosenblatt. An astonishing intellect sees works of literature as experiences, transactions involving author, text, and reader. Inspired by Rosenblatt, I derived a theory about the essential differences between reports and stories.

21. *Garner's Modern American Usage,* by Bryan A. Garner. The most popular and influential lexicon of American usage,

this work stands out for its reconciliation of descriptive and prescriptive approaches to language. It offers direction without making me feel like an imbecile.

22. *The John McPhee Reader,* by John McPhee, edited by William Howarth. More valuable than the selections of McPhee's early work is the introduction. Howarth describes in great detail McPhee's scrupulous working method, one that I borrowed to write my first book.

23. *A Writer's Reference,* by Diana Hacker. Every writer needs a spiral-bound text to remind him or her about the conventions of grammar, syntax, and punctuation. This one works for me.

24. *Wired Style,* by Constance Hale and Jessie Scanlon. Those of us who grew up with typewriters can benefit from this usage guide for the digital age.

25. *How Fiction Works,* by James Wood. The author shares the strategies of novelists for the benefit of every writer. Wood asks "a critic's questions" but offers "a writer's answers."

Additional resources for writers:

- The Poynter Institute website: www.poynter.org
- Online courses from News University: www.newsu.org
- Author's website: www.roypeterclark.com

Acknowledgments

—•—

I begin by acknowledging my continuing debt to the late Donald Murray, friend, mentor, and one of America's great writing teachers. I miss his imposing physical presence—white beard, red shirt, striped suspenders, and all—but his voice and spirit live on in his writings and in the work of his acolytes. He is quoted several times in this book, but his influence can be traced through every page.

I created the plan for *Help!* in about fourteen hours on a round-trip flight from Atlanta to Copenhagen. The idea was inspired by Julie Moos, editor of the journalism website Poynter.org, for which I write. A wonderful team of Poynter experts nurtured the idea. Keith Woods, Howard Finberg, and Julie Moos led the way. Casey Frechette and Ellyn Angelotti created a multimedia course for Poynter's News University. Steve Myers and the successfully homeschooled Leslie Passante have produced a mobile phone application. These Skunk Works adventures led us all to the same conclusion, that "hey, I think we've got a book here."

And so we did. Special thanks, as always, go to my agent, Jane Dystel, for her dogged representation. She has become one half of a dynamic duo of support for me, the other half being my editor Tracy Behar. This book completes an unofficial writing-and-language trilogy for the three of us. First came *Writing Tools,* then *The Glamour of Grammar,* and now *Help! For Writers.*

In an era when so many writers complain so loudly about their publishers, I have found working with Little, Brown to be a dream. Michael Pietsch has assembled a talented and dedicated team, which has included Keith Hayes, the award-winning cover designer; Betsy Uhrig, who, like her colleagues, has turned the craft of copyediting into an art form; proofreader Katie Gehron; and Sabrina Callahan, Michelle Aielli, Laura Keefe, and Christina Rodriguez, who have worked tirelessly to get the word out about my words.

On the home front, my love and thanks go to my mother, Shirley Clark, who at the age of ninety-two is thinking of setting up street tables on a Manhattan sidewalk to hawk my wares. To Karen, my wife of forty years, who better watch her step. To the three Weird Sisters, my daughters Emily, Lauren, and Alison, for having my back (so they can pinch my wallet). And to my buds Tom French, Jeff Saffan, my alter ego Go Go, Rex the dog, and the ladies at the Banyan restaurant, who know how to serve up to writers the Help! we most desperately need: strong coffee at the break of day.

INDEX

—•—

Index

Index

Index

About the Author

—•—

By some accounts, Roy Peter Clark is America's writing coach, a teacher devoted to creating a nation of writers. A PhD in medieval literature, he is widely considered the most influential writing teacher in the rough-and-tumble world of newspaper journalism. With a deep background in traditional media, Clark has illuminated the discussion of writing on the Internet. He has gained fame by teaching writing to children, and has nurtured Pulitzer Prize–winning authors such as Thomas French and Diana Sugg. He is a teacher who writes, and a writer who teaches.

For more than three decades, Clark has taught writing at the Poynter Institute, a school for journalists in St. Petersburg, Florida, considered among the most prominent such teaching institutions in the world. He graduated from Providence College in Rhode Island with a degree in English and earned a PhD from Stony Brook University.

In 1977 he was hired by the *St. Petersburg Times* to become one of America's first writing coaches and worked with the

American Society of Newspaper Editors to improve newspaper writing nationwide. Because of his work with ASNE, Clark was elected a distinguished service member, a rare honor for a journalist who has never edited a newspaper. He was inducted into the Features Hall of Fame, an honor he shares with the likes of Ann Landers.

Clark has authored or edited sixteen books about writing and journalism, including his most recent, *The Glamour of Grammar*. Humorist Dave Barry has said of him: "Roy Peter Clark knows more about writing than anybody I know who is not currently dead."

He lives with his family in St. Petersburg, Florida.